PENGUIN BOOKS
The Kiwi
Bible

Chris Grantham leads the New Zealand branch of an
international Christian development agency. Based in
Auckland, he gets out and about around New Zealand
with his speaking and writing, along with some stand-
up comedy here and there. After a couple of speaking
tours to South Africa, Chris is thinking of putting
'noted international speaker' on his CV. He's married
to Jocelyn, has a couple of grown-up kids, and in
previous lives was an accountant and schoolteacher.

Bits of . . .
The Kiwi
Bible

as told by
Chris Grantham

PENGUIN BOOKS

PENGUIN BOOKS
Published by the Penguin Group
Penguin Group (NZ), cnr Airborne and Rosedale Roads, Albany,
Auckland 1310, New Zealand (a division of Pearson New Zealand Ltd)
Penguin Group (USA) Inc., 375 Hudson Street,
New York, New York 10014, USA
Penguin Group (Canada), 10 Alcorn Avenue, Toronto,
Ontario, Canada M4V 3B2 (a division of Pearson Penguin Canada Inc.)
Penguin Books Ltd, 80 Strand, London, WC2R 0RL, England
Penguin Ireland, 25 St Stephen's Green,
Dublin 2, Ireland (a division of Penguin Books Ltd)
Penguin Group (Australia), 250 Camberwell Road, Camberwell,
Victoria 3124, Australia (a division of Pearson Australia Group Pty Ltd)
Penguin Books India Pvt Ltd, 11, Community Centre,
Panchsheel Park, New Delhi – 110 017, India
Penguin Books (South Africa) (Pty) Ltd, 24 Sturdee Avenue,
Rosebank, Johannesburg 2196, South Africa
Penguin Books Ltd, Registered Offices: 80 Strand, London, WC2R 0RL, England
First published by Penguin Group (NZ), 2005
1 3 5 7 9 10 8 6 4 2
Copyright © Chris Grantham, 2005

The right of Chris Grantham to be identified as the author of this work in terms of
section 96 of the Copyright Act 1994 is hereby asserted.

Designed by Mary Egan
Typeset by Egan Reid Ltd
Printed in Australia by McPherson's Printing Group

ISBN 0 14 302017 X

A catalogue record for this book is available
from the National Library of New Zealand.
www.penguin.co.nz

Contents

Introduction to
The Kiwi Bible

How on earth do you go about writing a Bible? It's a couple of millennia since the last major Bible-writing exercise took place, so this means there's currently a shortage of people who know how to put a Bible together. To be honest, this one isn't entirely original – it draws heavily on that other, better-known Bible. Matter of fact, mine is a much-reduced version of that particular Bible – just three per cent of the original. So if you actually *buy* this book rather than merely having a free bookshop lunchtime browse, who knows, there might be a sequel, or thirty even (yeah, right!) to cover the whole Bible.

Back to the story – it's been called the greatest story ever told, or, in Kiwi, a seriously good yarn. It's been a bestseller for several yonks. This particular small tome is not a genuine translation as such. I've got to be honest with you, I didn't spend long, sweaty hours poring over Greek papyri. Rather, I looked at a bunch of English-language translations and paraphrases and then had a shot at retelling it in Kiwi. Have a read, and you'll find the bloke Jesus turns out to be a very interesting character – much more so in fact than some of his subsequent salespeople have turned out to be. Don't hold that against them, he *is* a hard act to follow, and anyhow, God doesn't actually expect us to be *quite* as good as Jesus was. God's seen enough of us over the years to know that we do a fair amount of stuffing up along the road. And yet we get given another shot at it – good, eh? That's what Jesus is all about.

If you enjoy the story and reckon you'd like to know more, why not fork out a few more bucks and get the full version. Come to think of it, you can actually get the full million words for around what you paid for this edition. Be warned, though: there are lots of different models, and a new one seems to come along about as often as a new Windows operating system. If you like informal language, you could check out *The Message* version. It's not unlike *The Kiwi Bible*, except that it's very different, quite a few Americanisms etc, but nevertheless told well. Check out www.kiwibible.co.nz for ways of getting it – and various other versions too. Be warned, again, that some bookshops might only have Bibles that use old Shakespearian-type words – I reckon thou wouldst do best not to bother thyself with the forthwith acquisition thereof. If they sound like they're hundreds of years old, it's because they basically are!

When you put your name to a book it's fairly good practice to acknowledge a few mates – it helps to fill another page at least. So here goes. For starters, there are the guys at Ilam Baptist Church in Christchurch – they unwittingly were the first ones to hear *The Kiwi Bible* one Sunday way back last century. Then there's the team, Rachel King, Mary-Jane and Chris Konings, who read over my drafts and made helpful comments and corrections and so on, and helped me avoid embarrassing myself by telling me what certain words actually mean nowadays. Chris Marshall, an expert in biblical stuff, also cast a professional eye over it. Responsibility for any error or inaccuracy or whatever lies, of course, entirely with them (I think it's customary to say something like that at this point). Inspiration to get started came from Spike Milligan and his book *The Bible According to Spike Milligan*. And, of course, from God.

Geoff Walker and Rebecca Lal at Penguin have expertly guided me through the process – and they had enthusiastic confidence in the publication from the start. I'm most grateful!

Finally, thanks to my supportive family – Joce, who has bouncing-boarded throughout the various stages, plus our kids Mark and Rachel who have helped me keep my feet on the ground for a fair while now. And, oh yeah, all my other mates.

Go for it now, and may God help you to see something of Jesus, that really good bloke who can make things *so* worthwhile for you!

Chris Grantham
August 2005
Auckland, New Zealand (where else!)

Part One

The Jesus Stuff

Chapter 1

PREQUEL: ALL ABOUT HOW JESUS GOT STARTED

Mark, the guy who wrote the first version of most of this account, wasn't so much into the story of Jesus as a kid. He got straight into what Jesus did as an adult bloke. However, if we want the guff on what happened before that, our luck is in — a couple of Mark's mates known as Matt and Luke got the early stuff down on paper, so I've stuck this in here.

A different way of getting pregnant (Matt 1:18–25)

The birth of this bloke Jesus sort of happened like this. A woman called Mary got pregnant, but it happened a bit differently. Mary's fiancé Joseph had nothing to do with it – it was arranged sort of direct by God. Now, Joe wasn't so sure about all of this being right and proper. He was all set to send Mary off down the road when this angel character turned up in a dream one night when Joe was packing a few zzzs. This angel, she said, 'No worries Joe, God wants you to marry this woman, this baby bloke has been planted there direct by God, no worries. Matter of fact, you're going to call him Jesus and he's going to sort a few people out, OK?'

Joe woke up, he did, married Mary, but they didn't have it off till the little chap was born.

Meanwhile, down on the farm . . . (Luke 2:8-20)

Nearby, out in the neighbouring paddocks, there was a crowd of farmhands on night-time sheep-minding duties. While they were half nodding off, an angel turned up. This made quite an impact: it got incredibly bright – this was clearly something God was involved in – and it scared the pants off them. The angel reassured them: 'No worries you fellas! I've got some absolutely stunning news for you. Today, down the road in the town, this little nipper has been born. And he's no ordinary kid, he's going to make life totally rock! Cos, you see, he's God's special bloke. How do you know this is for real? Well, check out these details – he'll be dressed in typical baby stuff, but he'll be parked in a feeding box rather than your standard bassinet.'

Suddenly this humungous bunch of angels turned up alongside the original lone angel. Every one of them was enthusiastic. 'Wow, God's just fantastic!' they said. 'And around this place we trust you all have a happy Christmas, as it were.'

When the angels had taken off again, the farmworkers had a yarn: 'How about we head off down to Bethlehem, then we can see for ourselves this special kid God's rep just told us about.' Everyone agreed so they took to their heels. Sure as, they found Mary and Joe, and the wee bloke in the feeding box. They spread the news among their mates – and everyone was pretty well blown away by all accounts.

As for Mary, the kid's mum, she was stoked by all of this, and she kept chewing it over for a good while afterwards.

And the farmhands? Well, they went back to work, enthusiastically telling God how great they reckoned he was because of all the stuff they'd seen. What's more, it was word for word, frame by frame, *exactly* what they'd been told to expect.

A few smart blokes come for a look (Matt 2:1-11)

Now, at this particular stage in history when Jesus was born in Bethlehem, there was a guy called Herod who happened to be king. One day some smart researchers came wandering into town from some foreign parts. 'Where's this new mini-king of the Jews?' they asked. 'We saw his sign when we were studying the stars and stuff, and we've come to wet his head, as it were.'

Now, this sort of put the wind up the present monarch, and all his supporting cast too. He called the lawyers and religious leaders. 'Can you tell me where this special God character is supposed to be born?' he asked them.

'That's easy,' they told him. 'Bethlehem. The wise guys way back said so – they said: "Bethlehem, your number's going to be called, and you're going to produce a significant leader to guide the people around here." '

Herod summoned the smart blokes from – well, wherever – and asked them on the quiet when the particular star they were watching had started its notable journey. Having got the requisite guff from them, he sent them down the road to Bethlehem. 'Go and see if you can suss out where this little fellow is,' he told them. 'When you've got his location sorted, give me a bell, cos I'd like to go and be part of the celebrations too.'

The smart blokes acknowledged his request, and got their camels on the road again, following the said star till it came to a dead halt. They were stoked. 'This must be it!' they said. They entered the house and saw the kid there with Mary his mum, and they got down on their benders and worshipped the wee bloke. Then they opened the presents they'd brought along – a good heap of cash, some flash perfume, and some high-quality, reputable medicinal stuff.

Joe and co hit the road (Matt 2:12-23)

Goods delivered, the wee lad blessed and praised, it was time to hit the road again. But the smart blokes took the back roads this time because an angel told them it would be a good idea to keep away from Herod.

At this point an angel appeared to Joe (Mary's better half) in a dream. 'Get yourselves up and on the road to Egypt,' said the angel. 'When you get there, go to ground and stay there awaiting further instructions. Reason being, Herod (the miserable sod that he is) has got evil intent – he wants to do the kid in.'

That was more than enough encouragement for Joe. Middle of the night though it was, they got up and took off in the direction of Egypt. And they stayed there with a certain amount of normality till Herod kicked the bucket. This actually was in line with what one of the wise guys from way back had alluded to when he said, 'My lad is going to come out of Egypt.'

When old Herod heard that the smart blokes had taken him for a ride, well, he was pretty livid, yes sir he was! He told his security guys to nail every little boy under two in all of Bethlehem and its suburbs, to make sure he got the wee kid the smart blokes had been telling him about. In so doing, Herod was certainly confirming the prediction of Jerry, another wise guy from way back. Jerry's particular comments on this theme: 'There's going to be a fair amount of tears and crying and stuff. Mums are going to be really cut up long-term – because their kids have been knocked off.'

Eventually Herod shuffled off the planet when his number was called. Joe, now happily ensconced in Egypt, got another dream-time angel visitor. 'Time's up,' he told Joe. 'Pack your bags and head back up the road to Israel from where you started this particular journey. Thems that had it in for the lad, their earthly days have been terminated.'

So up Joe got and home he trot – with Mary and the kid in tow. On the way he got news that Herod's own lad had picked up the monarchical duties, which wasn't so good, knowing the sort of things the old man had got up to. He got some info from yet another dream, telling him to head out more to the sticks, to a one-camel town by the name of Nazareth. (Which was in fact exactly what another of the wise guys from way back had said would be the case.)

Chapter 2

GETTING THE SHOW
ON THE ROAD

John gets it all started (Mark 1:1-8)

Here goes – the story about Jesus, son of God. Good, eh?

Way, way back this bloke called Isaiah wrote, 'God says, "I'm going to send a bit of an advance guard to get things ready. He'll be doing some pre-event publicity, endeavouring to call attention to the fact that I'm on my way, so get yourselves organised." '

Sure enough, this guy John turned up, telling everyone it was about time they changed their crooked ways. People from round and about turned up to hear him, confessed their wrong stuff and got dunked in the local creek as a sign of a change. This John character was wild as, and a bit of a greenie. Wore all natural substances – and ate them too!

'Watch out you guys!' he said. 'If you think I'm all right, I'm just the supporting act. You wait for the main event. What I'm doing is just for starters really. The next guy will baptise with the real McCoy, God's Spirit. Yep, for sure!'

Jesus gets dunked, then has a hard time
(Mark 1:9-13)

Right on cue, Jesus turned up. He rolled up from that one-camel town known locally as Nazareth, and John dipped him in the creek. As he came up there was this great big bang/crash/flash and God's Spirit came upon him as a sort of dove lookalike. And this big voice boomed from above: 'You're my son, and a good lad at that, and I've got to tell you this: you really are all right!'

Next thing, the Spirit gave Jesus a bit of a push in the desert direction, and he hung out there for two days short of six weeks, during which time Satan gave him a fairly hard sort of run-around. There were all sorts of wild animals and stuff, but the angels kept an eye on him. Which is just as well as there's a fair bit more of the story to be told.

Jesus chooses a few blokes for his team
(Mark 1:14-20)

Now, John had been interrupted by the local cops, who'd locked him up. So Jesus decided it was his time to hit the road. 'Hey you guys,' he said. 'There's something up. God rules, OK? The times they are a-changing, and you'd better believe it's time you changed your lives around too.'

Jesus tramped along the Galilee waterfront and saw Simon and Andrew doing a spot of fishing to pay the mortgage. 'Join me,' he said. 'And let's work together at catching a lot better stuff than that.'

'Sounds like a good deal, we're in!' they replied.

So the three of them walked on, and what do you know, there were their mates the Zebedee boys – James and John – also getting ready for a fish. 'Join us!' Jesus called. And would you believe it, they did. Out of the boat, on the road, leaving their old man Zeb and the rest of the crew gobsmacked.

The action begins (Mark 1:21–35)

Anyhow, they walked on, got as far as this place Capernaum and, on the local equivalent of Sunday, turned up at the local equivalent of a church.[1] Guess who preached? Jesus! The locals were quite pleased actually, because he was heaps better than the usual speakers they got. A bloke there with a few problems caused by this evil spirit yelled out, 'Hey Jesus, what's up? Don't tell me you want to wipe us all out? You're God's special bloke, right?'

'Shut up and get out of him!' was Jesus' reply. And the evil force in the guy shook him right up, then quit with a blood-curdling yell. Talk about wow! The guys sitting around were quite taken with all of this. 'What's this, some new fad? Whatever, it sounds pretty all right. Good grief, even those awful spirit things get rolled.' As you can imagine, word got round and about pretty fast.

Meantime, Jesus and the lads decided it was time for refreshments, so they popped over to Simon and Andy's place for a drink. Now, Simon's mother-in-law was crook, and when they told Jesus this, he wandered in. He said, 'What's the story? Up you get.' And he took her by the hand and, yep, up she got. And she was right as rain. Which was pretty good, because then she went and got them all drinks.

Well, word got around as you might expect, and that night all the locals brought their sick mates and the ones with those evil spirits too. Jesus, of course, sorted them all out, but told the noisy demons to shut up and not spoil his work.

Jesus goes bush for a bit (Mark 1:36–39)

Next morning, crack of dawn – well, matter of fact, it was

---

1 It was actually Saturday, and it wasn't a church. It was in fact called a synagogue, sort of a parallel to a church. I've translated them into the nearest equivalent for Kiwis, who are more likely to do church on Sundays than synagogue on Saturdays.

probably a good few hours before that – Jesus crawled out of bed and headed bush to pray. At a more civilised hour, Simon and his mates woke up, discovered Jesus gone and, without even stopping for their Weet-Bix, headed out to find him. Which they did. 'Hey Jesus,' they said. 'Every joker and his dog is looking for you.'

'No worries,' said Jesus. 'Let's have a bit of variety today, there's a few other places in these parts that could do with some well-chosen words.' So they did just that, round and about all the local towns, with Jesus yarning to the people and telling those demons where to go.

When bits drop off (Mark 1:40-45)

On one such occasion there was this bloke with a common nasty skin condition which wasn't very nice. Bits kept dropping off him, you see, which meant nobody ever went near him. He said to Jesus: 'Hey man, I know you can fix me up if you want.' Jesus realised the guy was having a tough time of it. So he slapped the guy on the back in a caring kind of way, and said, 'No worries mate, you're good as new.' Wow! The guy was fixed, just like that. Jesus said, 'Now listen mate, for strategic reasons *please* don't go broadcasting this. Instead I want you to pop down to the minister at the local church and show him. Give him a few bucks, which will keep him happy too.'

But what do you know, the guy put the word out – and loudly too – on the grapevine. Now, this brought potential for considerable problems with the local authorities, plus the risk of everyone with headaches, crook knees and ingrown toenails – in fact, just about any ailment you can think of, real or imagined – turning up for a cure. So Jesus kept off the busy routes, but they still found him.

Bringing down the house, sort of (Mark 2:1-12)

A couple of days later, Jesus popped back to Capernaum. And

for Capernaum this was a big deal. Jesus was chatting to some blokes at their flat, and the place got totally filled with humanity – apparently all busting to hear what he had to say. Talk about squashed! But wait, there's more . . . These four guys came along with their mate who was a paraplegic. They were carrying him, actually, wheelchairs not having yet been invented. Now, as I already said, the place was chocker. What to do? 'No worries. There's a roof, ain't there?' noted one of the four guys.

So up they went, dragging their mate with them, and with a bit of bang-crash-scrape-and-dig they created a new skylight. By the time they dangled the guy down, Jesus had wiped the surprise – and the bits of ceiling – from his face. 'Now *that's* a bit of faith if I ever saw any!' exclaimed Jesus. 'Hey son, your sin and stuff – it's gone, no worries.'

'Who the hell does he think he is?' asked some of the local God squad, who'd been watching Jesus with a wary eye. 'Only God can forgive sins, for crying out loud.'

Jesus could see right through those guys. 'I can see right through you guys,' he told them. 'What's the big deal? Tell me this, is it easier to say to this bloke "Your sin's gone", or "Get on your feet mate and go for a run"? But just to show you that I'm in good with God on this stuff . . .' He turned to the paraplegic and said, 'Get on your feet mate and go for a run.' The now ex-paraplegic did just that, and as you can imagine this was quite impressive. 'Good God, you're all right,' they said. 'That's quite original!'

The taxman joins up (Mark 2:13–17)

Time for another wander down at the waterfront and a spot of fresh air. But of course the locals all came for the ride, so he spouted some good and sensible stuff to them as they walked. They passed the various craft stalls and New Age purveyors and bumped into Matt (a.k.a. Levi) doing his dodgy mobile tax assessments. 'Forget that stuff, join *us*,' Jesus told him. And blimey, he did!

Jesus scored a feed at Matt's place that night. Matt had invited a whole crowd of his money-grabbing mates, skanks and druggies over to meet Jesus and co, and the Bible-bashers didn't think too much of that. 'Look at him,' they said. 'Knocking it back with that bunch of write-offs!'

'Stop your whingeing, you guys,' Jesus told them. 'This bunch are interested in what I have to offer – whereas you lot, you're basically up yourselves.' With that he moved on, wise man that he was.

To eat or not to eat? (Mark 2:18-22)

Remember John the greenie bloke from a couple of pages back? Well, some of his mates and other religious types were on one of those trendy no-food diets with lots of praying. 'How come *your* mates aren't into that?' someone asked Jesus.

'Cos it's a stupid diet combo when it's party season,' Jesus replied. 'When the party's over, then they'll give the no-food-and-pray-lots thing a spin. No one wears fancy gear with crappy patches on it. No one puts a decent bubbly into a cheap paper cup.'

Does it matter what day it is? (Mark 2:23-3:6)

One Sunday Jesus took a shortcut through the shopping mall, and his mates grabbed a moment to get a few supplies. Some of the miserable religious sods took exception to that, Sunday shopping being frowned on in those days. 'For crying out loud!' Jesus told them. 'In the old days when David and his troops were nearly dying of hunger, they found a bit of bread and wine in the church – which they scoffed (the bread and wine that is, not the church). A good thing to do, if you ask me. Listen you dorks, when it comes to doing good, me and God don't give a stuff what day of the week it is.'

Another time Jesus wandered into the local (church, that is) and there was this fellow with a hand that was rather inadequate in the useful department, to say the least. The religious guys watched Jesus to see if he'd fix the guy's hand on a Sunday, this being a right no-no in their book. Jesus, as you might guess, takes the bait – or ignores it, depending on how you look at it. Anyhow, he tells the bloke, 'OK you, stand up where we can all see you.'

Then he turns and addresses everyone in general and no one in particular: 'What do you reckon goes down best on Sundays? Good stuff or stupid stuff? Giving a bloke a helping hand or kicking him in the guts?' Well, of course that caught them on the hop, so they said nix.

But that got Jesus a bit wild. The miserable sods, he thought to himself. So he said to the bloke with the crook hand, 'Here, gizza decent look at your hand.' Well, believe it or not, when he stuck out his hand it was as good as new! The religious guys were totally cheesed off at that, and they took to their heels – deciding as they did so to team up with another bunch (the Herod gang) who also had it in for Jesus.

Chapter 3

JESUS DOES LOTS OF STUFF AROUND THE HOME PATCH

Jesus picks his team (Mark 3:7-19)

Jesus, meanwhile, took off down to the beach for a breather. Some hope! Because, as was happening plenty, people from hither and yon came for the ride – or the walk, more correctly. They'd heard about the sort of stuff he got up to, and on a quiet Sunday afternoon why not join the action? He got his mates to organise a dinghy (at this point he wasn't into going for a stroll across the top) so as to avoid getting squashed by the crowd. He'd fixed up a fair swag of them by this time, and everywhere people with a few bugs or whatever were just about crowding him out. There were a few with evil spirits and stuff too – and the spooks sort of knew Jesus had a hotline to God and shouted it out rather loudly. Which didn't please Jesus, who told them in no uncertain terms to shut up.

A bit later, Jesus headed for the hills and took some of his mates with him. While up there he picked out a dozen who he reckoned would do all right as sort of apprentices, a kind of focus group. It's worth dropping their names in at this point, especially as some don't get much coverage later in the story. There was Simon who Jesus later called Peter (which means 'rock', and was quite apt as Peter was inclined to be a bit thick at times). Then there were James and John, old Zeb's lads who were in the fishing trade. Jesus called them 'sons of thunder' as they did sound off a bit like thunder at times. Then – where were we? – that's right, there was Andrew (Simon's kid brother), Phil, Bart, Matt, Thomas and another James (Alf was his old man). That leaves Thad, another Simon, and Judas – which is not a name in common usage these days. Later on we'll see why.

That job done, they popped home for some kai – but the crowds got in the road somewhat and they couldn't get hold of as much as a Moro bar. Now, his family weren't too excited about all of this. 'Has he lost his marbles?' they asked, wondering if he was getting a bit carried away or up himself or something.

Who is Jesus anyhow? (Mark 3:20-35)

A bunch of religious academics turned up at that point and stirred the pot a tad. 'He's doing his stuff with more than a bit of black magic,' they reckoned. (This stuff was definitely frowned upon in the days before Harry Potter.)

Jesus ripped into them. 'For crying out loud, why the hell would the devil toss out the devil? That would be straight stupid! If the devil has a punch-up with the devil, eventually we'd be quite short in the devil department. If a housebreaker wants to do a job when the owner's at home, he's not going to get far unless he punches out the owner's lights or similar – only then is the stuff his for the taking, and he can nick anything he wants.

'Get a handle on this,' said Jesus, warming to his point. 'You can get forgiven a right swag of stuff. But if you don't take God's long-term representative seriously, well, you've good as got the skids under you permanent-like – which should really put the wind up you.' (Some of them, you see, were saying Jesus was, as it were, in the pocket of the devil.) This probably wiped the grin off a few of their faces.

Anyhow, that was an opportune time for Jesus' mum and siblings to turn up. 'Hey Jesus, your whanau is here to see you,' they called.

'Hear that?' the crowd asked Jesus. 'Your mum and kid bros are here.'

'Oh yeah?' replied Jesus. 'Me mum and me bros? I tell you what – *you* lot are me mum and me bros and me sisters. Yep, that's right. If you do the stuff God has in mind, then you're the same as me own flesh and blood.'

A farming story (Mark 4:1–20)

Another time, Jesus was spouting some good sense down at the beach. As usual the place got full as, so he got into this conveniently handy dinghy, which acted as a sort of floating stage. Being quite a good storyteller he did some quite good storytelling of quite a few stories, always with a good punchline. Like this one, for example:

'A bloke decided to put down a bit of a crop of edible stuff. Instead of doing it sensibly he just sort of tossed the seeds about hither and yon. Some landed on the patio where the sparrows got them. Others landed on the edge of the path where the dirt was in short supply, and they were goners in no time. Still other seeds got confused with the weed department, and of course the weeds were better growers – which is why they're called weeds. Curtains to that lot. And a few of them landed in the rich soil and bingo, up they grew – and a fantastic paddock-load of carrots it was too. You know what I'm getting at?' Jesus asked them.

Enough for now, thought Jesus, and took off with some of his mates, including his twelve best ones. 'You tell an all right story,' they told him. 'But we're sometimes missing the punchline, as it were. Like, what do you actually *mean*?'

Jesus said, 'Hey you guys have got a bit of potential, so I'll spill the beans and give you God's lowdown. That other lot,' he said, nodding back in the direction they had come from, 'are a bit slow, as a matter of fact. While they reckon they can see this sort of stuff all right, they're actually blind as, and a bit deaf too, figuratively speaking. Otherwise they'd change and get their lives sorted for the better. All right you guys, are you going to listen with your brains? Cos if you don't you'll miss the rest of the plot too.

'The guy flinging the seeds around is like someone with a spot of good news and he tells the news to a range of people at, like, a party. The ones on the patio – well, they've scarcely heard the news when someone comes out and offers them another drink, and wham, the news is gone. The ones on the edge of the path – they're a bit like the couple of blokes strolling down the driveway who are in the middle of a good joke when the news gets delivered, and they half notice the news then get back to the joke. Then there are the ones that landed among the weeds and got outsmarted. They're a bit like those who are bogged down at work and, though they're at the party, they still can't stop thinking about their work, and the news quickly gets buried under some problematic work issue. Finally there are the seeds that went straight over the fence and landed fair-square in the dirt where they ought to have gone. They're like the people who hear the good news, get enthusiastic about it, change their lives around a bit to suit, and tell all their mates. Nice one!'

Other stories about God's great outfit
(Mark 4:21–34)

Jesus carried on, warming to his subject. 'If a bloke goes eeling at night, does he stick his torch up his jacket? Stupid git if he did, eh? No way, he lets the light do its thing – and that's the point of

28

enlightening stuff, don't you see? If you've got half a brain you can see the point. Get it?' There was no answer.

He concluded, 'You'd be a bit stupid if you didn't get a grasp of what I'm saying. Don't get up yourself, cos others will show you up and get the better of you. And then you'll have nothing, right? Whereas if you listen and get this stuff, then there'll be more wise stuff for you.'

Jesus had another idea. 'God's outfit is a bit like when another bloke tosses some seed in the dirt, puts up his feet for forty winks, and forgets all about the seed. You'll be guessing what happens – it grows, of course. However, this particular bloke has forgotten all about it – yet it still grows. Of course it doesn't need *him*. It happens just like that. And before long he's got a great patch of broccoli or whatever, which he proceeds to dig up.'

While they were still thinking about the broccoli and carrots stories, Jesus had another thought. 'This outfit of God's, how can we best describe it? Well, it's like a pohutukawa seed which grows into a tree we can all have a picnic under. The seed is tiny, and does its stuff quietly – but wow, what an impact the finished product makes. Awesome!'

Jesus told them story after story, bang bang bang! They liked it, and it sort of suited the types of people they were. After storytime he'd have a bit more of a yarn with his close mates and tell them what the stories actually meant. It was quite good being in the know.

One hell of a storm (Mark 4:35–41)

Day's over, night's here. Jesus says to his mates, 'Hey guys, let's go across the other side, eh?' So they took off, leaving the crowd in their wake, with the odd observer boat tagging along. They were out in the middle when one hell of a storm hit them. Water everywhere, and seemingly forgetting what side of the boat it was supposed to be on. Talk about sink – man, they were that close. While this went on, Jesus, believe it or not, was having a bit of a kip down the back. Well, his mates didn't think too much of *that*, and shook him awake. 'Listen boss,' they said, 'we're about to drown and you give all the appearance of not giving a stuff!'

Jesus was rather unimpressed with that remark, and equally unimpressed with the weather. He got up, turned to face the elements, and quite simply said, 'Shut up!' And just like that, the wind *did* shut up. End of story.

Turning to his mates, he said, 'Well lads, *now* what do you say? Still don't trust me?'

They sort of freaked out at that. 'Good grief!' they blurted out. 'Who on earth *is* this guy? He tells the wind and waves and stuff what to do, and they do it.'

Who the devil is this? (Mark 5:1-20)

After that they headed across the lake to this place which was called something that sounded like Kerosene. When Jesus got out of the boat, this bloke who had the devil in him appeared from his pad down at the cemetery. Man, he was wild as. You couldn't hold him down with anything, that's for sure. A few guys had given it a go, but no way, he broke everything – ropes, chains, blokes' arms, the lot.

Mostly people kept very well away from him, you can put your dollar on that. All day, all night, he'd wander around the cemetery and thereabouts yelling and screaming and doing himself injuries on the rocks.

Then Jesus turned up nearby and, well, this guy ran right up to him. 'Hey Jesus!' he yelled as loud as. 'You're God's kid for sure. But what are you wanting from me? For God's sake, *please* don't do me over!' (He said that because Jesus had just said to this evil spirit in him, 'Hey you – clear off, get lost!')

Anyhow, Jesus said to him, 'What's your name, mate?'

The bloke replied, 'They call me Helluvalot, cos there's a helluvalot of us spirits in here.'

Then Helluvalot asked Jesus umpteen times to please, *please* not send them packing. Now, it happened that nearby there was a whole bunch of pigs – make that a *herd* of pigs – pigging out, as it were. And these spirits said to Jesus, 'How about we go into them pigs for want of anywhere better to go?'

'Done!' said Jesus – and yep, those spirits took off and took up residence in the pigs. This was not so good for the pigs. They took to their trotters and went charging over the edge of the cliff, straight down into the drink. Two grand of them there were, and every last one drowned.

The guys who were previously managing the pigs found themselves short of work at this point – so they took off and told all the locals what had happened. And all the locals showed up to see what was going on – this stuff sounding quite interesting. When they got there they saw Jesus and old Helluva – he was sitting there normal like, sweet as, no worries. Wow, that put the wind up them a bit. The eyewitnesses told the new arrivals what had happened to Helluva – and then what had happened to the herd of pigs.

'Hey you!' they said to Jesus. 'Clear off, you're bad for business.'

Jesus cleared off – he went back down to the boat. And guess who turned up? Old Helluva! He was keen to come for the ride, Jesus having made a fair difference to him as you can imagine. But Jesus told him, 'Sorry mate, this trip's not for you. What I want you to do is head home to your folks and tell them what God has done, eh? That'll keep you busy in a good cause.' So the man formerly known as Helluva did just that – took off and told everyone in the local towns just what God had done for him. And I tell you, the people were quite impressed.

Sick, dead or both? (Mark 5:21–43)

Meantime, Jesus headed back across the lake. Solitude? No way – a large bunch had got themselves together there. A guy from the local church-type place turned up. This guy (Jairus by name) saw Jesus and fell down on the ground. He didn't trip, it was what you did when you respected somebody. Anyhow, he said to Jesus, 'Hey man, me kid's about to kark it. Can you come and see her and get her fixed up so that she'll be right as?'

'No worries bro,' said Jesus. 'Let's go!' And they went, but not just the two of them – the whole swag of people who were there, all of them. Now, in the crowd was this woman who'd had, well, women's problems, and for twelve years straight. She'd had it pretty rough, seen the whole medical profession it seemed, and some of them had been a straight rip-off too. Now she hadn't a dollar left. Totally broke. And she was still crook, like having a permanent monthly.

Anyhow, this woman had heard about Jesus, so she pushed through the crowd and sneaked up behind him. 'All I need to do is touch the back of his jacket, then I'll be right,' she said to herself. So she touched the back of his jacket. Man alive – *immediately* she stopped bleeding, and felt heaps better.

Jesus was a fairly clued-up guy, and he felt some vibes. 'Hey, who touched my jacket?' he asked.

'Come off it,' his mates replied. 'There's stacks of people pushing and shoving, and yet you actually say, "Who did that?" You've got to be joking, man!' Jesus wasn't put off by that. He knew better, and kept looking around. This woman could see that – and she knew who he was looking for. She fell down on the ground (she didn't trip – as you've already heard, it was what you did when you respected somebody). And she told Jesus the whole story.

'Well I never,' he said to her in a kindly way. 'That's some sort of faith if I've ever seen it. Good on you too – cos it's fixed you up good and proper. Go for it, and have a nice life!'

Jesus hadn't even caught his breath when some of Jairus' mates rolled up. 'The kid's karked it,' they said. 'No need to bother this guy any more.'

Jesus just ignored them, and told Jairus, 'No worries mate,

believe me and she'll be sweet as.' Apart from Pete, James and his bro John, Jesus told the rest of the crowd to scatter. At Jairus' place there was a whole bunch of people bawling their eyes out, and doing it loudly too. 'What's with all the racket?' he asked them. 'She ain't dead, she's only having a bit of shut-eye.'

'Yeah, right!' they said. 'Who are you kidding?' Jesus didn't bother replying, but he cleared everyone out of the house, and then went into the kid's bedroom – just him, his three mates and her olds. He took the kid by the hand and said, 'Hey girl, up you get.' Guess what? Up she got! Well, you could have knocked them down with a feather.

'Now listen everybody,' Jesus told them. 'I'd be obliged if you'd keep the details of what happened here absolutely confidential, OK?' With that clarified, Jesus suggested it might be a good idea to give the girl a feed.

The locals take Jesus for granted (Mark 6:1-6)

Jesus and his mates left – well, they left wherever they happened to be at the time. They headed down to Jesus' home patch, that small outfit called Nazareth. It was Sunday, so they popped in to the local church, and as luck would have it, Jesus happened to be the one sitting nearest the pulpit. So, you're right, he was the day's preacher. And, wow, did he blow them away. 'That sounds pretty all right,' they said. But all the same, they were just a bit on the concerned side. 'Where on earth did he come up with this?' they asked. 'What's he got that lets him do all these smart things? And, we say this in a non-discriminatory way, isn't he just a chippie? Hey, ain't that his old lady over there? We know his sisters and his bros, and, well, they're OK, but really, who the blazes does he really think he is?'

Jesus was a bit brassed off at that kind of reaction. 'It's always your rellies and your old mates who give you the hardest time,' he said. While there were a few there who were prepared to give him the time of day, most of them weren't. So when he'd helped some of them and got them fixed up, Jesus and his mates just cleared out of town. They decided instead to pop in on a few of the people living on the other side of the track.

Jesus' mates get to do stuff (Mark 6:7-13)

After a while Jesus said to his mates, 'Hey guys, I've done quite a bit of stuff with you just sort of looking on. I want you to head out on your first proper field trip. I want you to team up with a mate, and you can be sure you've got my authority over the evil stuff.' Jesus then gave them some working rules for the trip: 'I want you to travel real light, so just take the basics. You'll fit all you need in a day-pack. Backpackers' places will be as much luxury as you need. If you find anywhere that the locals give you the cold shoulder and act as if you don't exist, well, don't hang around there. Move on to where they *do* appreciate what you've got to offer.'

With that, Jesus packed them out the door and on their way. The guys took well to the task, doing the sort of stuff they'd seen Jesus doing. They told the locals it would be real good to get their lives sorted out, they fixed up those who were crook, and of course they dealt to the evil forces.

Chapter 4

QUITE A BIT OF LEARNING FOR JESUS' MATES

John and his head part company (Mark 6:14–29)

Meantime, back at the palace, Herod (who was the local king at the time)[2] heard about some of what Jesus was up to – Jesus had become quite an event round the neighbourhood. 'Hey you guys,' some of them said, 'that guy John who was dunking everyone in the river – looks like he's back *this* side of the cemetery, must be *him* doing all that flash stuff.'

Others reckoned it was probably Elijah from way back. Still others thought he was a new wise guy (like the sorts who used to hang around hundreds of years ago).

Old Herod, however, had no doubt. 'It's that guy John, for sure,' he reckoned. 'Even though I had his head removed from his shoulders, he's back alive!'

---

2   Remember, this Herod was not the same bloke who was king when
    Jesus was a nipper. In fact, it was one of that particular Herod's lads,
    also called Herod, who was now running the show.

We need a bit of a flashback here.

Some time back, Herod had got John picked up and thrown in the slammer. Why? Because John had told Herod upfront that marrying Herodias – who was already married to Herod's bro – was not on. As you can imagine, Herodias didn't have too much time for John and would have loved to put a contract on him. However, Herod thought John was an all right sort of customer and in with the good oil, well worth listening to he was. So Herod's missus knew she couldn't have John done in just like that.

But one day her moment came. It happened like this: it was Herod's birthday and he threw this mighty bash for all the bigwigs from all over. Herodias' daughter turned up, and man, could she dance. As you can imagine, Herod and all his mates were pretty impressed by that. 'Hey girl!' said Herod, who'd probably had a few. 'What can I get you? Anything you ask for, *anything*, and it's yours. Matter of fact,' he added, probably to show his mates that he was a powerful sort of bloke, 'you can even have half of this whole outfit!' He waved his hand generally in the direction of all the territory he was kingpin of.

She ducked out to get a spot of advice from her mum. 'Hey Mum!' she said excitedly. 'Your bloke has said he'll give me anything I ask for. *Anything*! Whaddaya reckon?'

Quick as a flash, Mum replied, 'Ask him for that guy John's head.'

So she went back into the party and said to Herod, 'I've chosen. I want that guy John's head served up on a platter. That's all.' Now that put the wind up Herod for sure – he certainly wasn't anticipating *that* request. He knew he'd painted himself into a corner – and, what's more, he didn't want to look like a wuss with all his mates watching on with considerable interest. So he sent one of the security guys off to the jail with instructions to bring back John's head – minus the rest of him. Shortly thereafter, John's head arrived on a large plate. Security gave it to the girl – and she fairly quickly handed it over to Mum.

John's mates, of course, were totally gutted by this when they got word. But they came and got his body and gave him a decent funeral.

Now we can get back into the main story – the above was so as you'd know why Herod was talking about John being dead and maybe coming back. You can understand now why he was a bit freaked out at the idea of John being up and about and back in town, when last time he'd seen him it was just the head bit.

Jesus takes up catering (Mark 6:30-44)

Jesus' mates got back from their time on the road, all set for a bit of a debrief. They told him everything, no holds barred. After they'd finished – and that took a fair time – Jesus told the guys, 'Hey, there's so many people round here we can't even hear ourselves think, never mind get any kai. Let's clear off for a bit of a breather, eh?'

So they waved down a passing boat and took off to a quiet spot further round the lake. Trouble was, some of the smart ones in the crowd guessed where they were heading, and would you believe it, took to their heels and got there first. So by the time Jesus and his mates got out of the boat, there was already quite a crowd there. Jesus could see they were a rather needy bunch of almost no-hopers – he knew that nobody else could be bothered giving them any pointers for doing a bit better out of life. So he stood, shushed the crowd, and told them a few helpful home truths.

This went on for a while, in fact it got quite late, and Jesus' mates *still* hadn't had a feed. To be honest, they were feeling half starved. 'Hey Jesus,' they said, 'send that lot on their way to the takeaways or whatever so that they can have a feed. Then we can grab a bite too.'

'You lazy sods!' said Jesus. '*You* give 'em something to eat.'

'You gotta be joking!' they replied. 'To feed a crowd like that wouldn't leave any spare out of twenty grand. Which, in case you hadn't noticed, we don't actually have.'

'All righty,' said Jesus. 'Do you have *any* grub at all? Go for a quick look-see.'

Which they did. 'Um, Jesus,' they said, 'it's not what you'd call much of a meal. There's five loaves of bread with a couple of fish thrown in for good measure. Now *that's* not gonna go far, eh?'

Ignoring his mates' pessimism, Jesus told them to sit the people down on the grass in an orderly sort of way, not just in a jumbled heap. He then picked up the bread and the fish (which were so small you could scarcely see them), and looked up into the sky. He wasn't thinking, Good grief, what now? but rather thanking God for them. Then he handed them over to his mates and said, 'Hey, spread that lot around, and you'll find there's enough for a good feed for everyone.'

Well, believe it or not, everyone – and there were maybe fifteen thousand of them – got stoked up and said it was the best feed they'd had for ages, and there was still buckets of food left over afterwards. Good stuff, eh!

The water's not for sinking (Mark 6:45–56)

After tea, Jesus told his mates to get back into the boat and head round to another town, so off they went. Meanwhile, Jesus told the crowd, 'That's it for the day, time to go, catch you next time.'

Then he hiked up the nearest hill to have a bit of a pray. It was dark by now, he was praying, and the boys were out there rowing the dinghy. Jesus could see them in the distance, and as the wind was coming up rather worryingly, they were having a spot of bother. Jesus, being a compassionate sort of bloke, headed down the hill and started hiking across the lake – which wasn't a particularly common activity in those days. He was just about to stroll on past them, but they saw him and were a bit spooked – and they yelled out in a fairly frightened tone of voice.

Jesus realised this. 'Hey you guys, it's me, Jesus, no worries.' He climbed into the dinghy, and believe it or not, the wind stopped dead in its tracks.

'Well, blow me down!' they said. 'We're still trying to understand how you fed that lot with a couple of whitebait and five bread rolls – and now you're strolling across the waves! What are you on?' Now, that was a bit of a rhetorical question because they knew Jesus was trying to show them bit by bit something which they couldn't yet get a hold of.

Eventually they got over to the shore at yet another reserve, hoping for a chance for their guts to settle down. But – you guessed it – the ubiquitous crowds materialised out of nowhere yet again. They'd picked it was Jesus, and many of them had already seen some of his acts. People came from all over bringing their mates who were sick, half dead or even worse. They were yelling out stuff like: 'Hey boss, all we need to do is touch your jacket and we'll be sorted.' And they did – and they were (sorted, that is).

Rules and stupid rules (Mark 7:1-23)

A bunch of the God-botherers turned up from down the road in Jerusalem, and they happened to notice that when Jesus' mates had a feed, they didn't wash their hands in the way proper religious people did back then. No sir, this wasn't on. These God-botherers used to do it real proper-like, cleaning all the plates and cutlery and stuff till it shone like nothing on earth.

'Hey Jesus,' they said to him. 'How come your mates don't do it our way, but get stuck straight into a feed without so much as going past the tap?'

Jesus took a dim view of their approach. 'The old guy Isaiah sure had your sorts sussed when he said, "This lot can make all the right noises, but it makes no difference deep down to the right sods that they really are. They actually say that I'm an all-round great guy, but it doesn't make a scrap of difference – they still make up their own stupid rules." You guys,' Jesus told them, 'have made up your own rules and conveniently forgotten the ones God gave you!'

He continued, 'Old Moses said respect your olds or you're history. But you lot? You try to get out of your obligations by saying whatever you might have bothered to do for your olds is actually for God. You pikers! In effect you're saying you've no time for the good book – you'd rather go with the flow. I'm sorry to say that this seems to be your general approach to stuff.'

Jesus called the crowd back from their wanderings round and about and said, 'Listen you lot. What you eat isn't what makes a right sod of you. It's what you say and do that can stuff up everything.' Later on, when the crowds had had enough for the day and everyone had gone back to their own pad, Jesus' mates said to him, 'Sorry to sound thick boss, but we're not quite sure we got your last points this afternoon. Could we have a quick recap?'

'Come on!' Jesus replied. 'Are you guys totally thick – or is that just the impression you're trying to give? It's not the stuff you feed yourself with that decides whether you're a good bloke or a right sod.' (In telling them that, Jesus was basically saying pretty well any food's OK for you, no worries.) 'What marks you out as a bad egg is all the stuff you say and do that you shouldn't. You know, stuff like nicking what ain't yours, running off with some other bloke's woman, behaving like an absolute dork, getting boozed, killing someone even – all of that and more. It's that kind of stuff which you've got deep down in you that's the problem, that's for sure.'

Jesus fixes up some more crook people
(Mark 7:24-37)

While they were still thinking on that, Jesus upped and took off to another town. He snuck into a house for a bit of peace and quiet, but the usual crowds soon had his whereabouts sussed. There was this immigrant woman whose kid daughter had this evil force thing. 'Hey boss!' she called out to Jesus. 'Would you mind getting this horrible thing out of me kid?'

'First things first,' Jesus told her. 'Let the kids have their lunch. Only then can the dogs have theirs.' (By this he was referring to the fact that God's intention was to get the Jews onside for starters, and after that work with everyone else, including her particular lot.)

'Sure thing,' she replied, realising what Jesus was getting at. 'But the dogs can still get their feed from the crumbs under the table!'

'You're not stupid,' Jesus said. 'Because you're so on to it, it's all done. The force has gone. Your daughter's sweet as!' So she took off home, and sure thing, her daughter *was* sweet as.

Jesus moved off, passed through this place called Sidon, and headed back down to the beach. Some locals turned up with their mate – he was deaf as a post and couldn't get a word out either. Jesus took this guy aside and, would you believe, he poked him in the ear, then spat on his finger and put it on the guy's tongue! He then looked up, prayed something, and said to the guy, 'Hey, open up, mate.' Guess what – the man immediately could hear, and he could speak plain as day too.

Being more than a tad publicity-shy, Jesus asked them to keep it hushed up. Yeah, right! The more he did, the more they told all their mates. 'He's done all right,' they said. 'Good grief, he gets the deaf hearing and the dumb yabbering. Choice, eh?'

More catering (Mark 8:1-9)

Some time later another crowd got together – Jesus being the centre of attraction as per usual. They'd been there for a fair while, and were actually feeling half starved. So Jesus called to his mates and said, 'Hey you guys, I feel just a smidgen sorry for this lot. They've been here for three days, would you believe, and not so much as a crumb has passed their lips. If I suggest they clear off home that would be the miserablest thing I could do. Some of them live absolutely miles away, and they'd keel over.'

'Fair enough,' replied his mates. 'But just where do you suggest in this café-free shop-forsaken spot we get them a feed?'

'Haven't you got *anything*?' Jesus asked them.

'Well yeah, seven loaves of bread, that's it,' they answered.

'Hey you lot, sit down, eh,' Jesus told them. He took the bag of bread, thanking God for it as you can imagine. He then broke it up into little bits and handed it all over to his mates, who acted as waiters. Along with the bread there were a few fish, so they handed them out as well – fish sandwiches were clearly the catch of the day. Would you believe, there were seven buckets of leftovers – his mates knew that because they were on tidying-up duty as well. All up, some four thousand blokes shared in the meal. Throw in all the women and kids and it must have been a good twelve thousand all told.

After-dinner reflections (Mark 8:10–21)

With the crowd fed and watered, Jesus could now send them on their way, which he did. He and his mates then caught another ferry conveniently passing at the time, and headed down the road, figuratively speaking. They arrived and parked the boat, then ran into a few of the God squad who took the opportunity to throw some curly questions at Jesus, hoping to catch him out.

'Hey,' Jesus responded, 'why are you lot always looking for some fancy sign? I tell you what, you ain't getting one, you can stick it.'

With that, he got back into the boat with his mates and they headed to the other side of the lake. Even though it was getting on for lunchtime, his mates, who he'd asked to keep an eye on the catering department, of course had forgotten. All a quick whip-round turned up was one miserable bread roll and no fish. 'Watch out for the yeast in that religious lot and the royalists,' Jesus warned them.

'What's he on about?' they asked each other. 'Presumably he's noticed we forgot the bread – again!'

'You guys,' said Jesus, 'are thick as. Can't you use your heads for once? I'm not talking about food, for crying out loud. Remember when I provided a feed for that bunch of fifteen thousand? How much was left over?'

'Let's see, ah, twelve baskets, eh?' they responded.

'Bang on!' said Jesus, encouragingly. 'What about the twelve thousand who've just had their feed – what did you collect after?'

'Seven buckets,' they told him.

'Now do you see what I'm getting at?' Jesus asked them. Dead silence. Clearly they didn't.

I can't see clearly now (Mark 8:22-26)

They moved on down the track, and some of the locals brought out this blind guy to see Jesus (well, he couldn't see, that was the problem). 'Would you fix this guy up, please?' they asked Jesus. So he took him by the arm to a quieter spot, spat in his eyes (in a kind and caring way, mind you), touched them and then asked, 'Well, see anything?'

'Um, yeah,' the bloke replied. 'I can see a few people, but they actually look a bit like trees having a stroll.'

So Jesus had another go, touching the guy's eyes again. 'Now what?' he asked him. Guess what, the guy could see everything perfect-like. Good, eh? Jesus gave him a pat on the back and sent him off, saying, 'Go for a walk mate, and I suggest you keep away from your home and neighbours for a bit.'

Chapter 5

HEADING IN THE DIRECTION OF TROUBLE

Pete susses out who Jesus is (Mark 8:27-30)

'OK boys,' Jesus told his mates, 'let's go for a bit of a walk.'
While they were walking, he said to them, 'Hey you guys, who
do people reckon I am?'

'Well, some of them say you're that guy John who used to
dunk people in the river. Others reckon you're Elijah from way
back. And others reckon you're really smart as,' they answered.

Jesus looked straight at them. 'Let's get even more specific.
Who do *you* guys reckon I am?'

Pete replied, quick as, 'You're God's number one bloke, the
one that everyone's been waiting for!'

'Hey guys, I want you to breathe not a word of that to
anybody, not a soul, OK?' Jesus told them.

Jesus sees death down the track (Mark 8:31-9:1)

Jesus then got real serious, and told his mates that as God's special agent he was going to get it fairly rough – that all the religious types had got it in for him. He was going to get taken out – but guess what, in three days he'd be back!

Pete didn't like the sound of all this, no sir. 'Listen mate,' he told Jesus, 'that'll be quite enough of that sort of carry-on.'

Jesus, however, wasn't going to have a bar of Pete's approach, no way. 'Carry on like that Pete, and you can take a running jump. You just don't get it, do you? You're so focused on trivia that you just don't get the big picture that God's trying to show you.'

He turned to the crowd that seemed to have materialised around his mates as per usual, and said to them all, 'Listen you lot. If you want to be part of my crowd, then you've gotta do things my way. It's going to be tough as, totally life-threatening even. But man, if you want to really live, then this is the only way you can do it. It might sound wacky, but it's an approach worth dying for, promise you that.

'Put it another way,' he continued. 'What the blazes is the point of getting absolutely loaded with everything money can buy and then some, and then at the end of the day sort of vaporising? A particularly stupid trade-off if there ever was one. Listen you guys, if you ignore what I'm telling you, it's going to be the stupidest thing you ever did. Why? Because God's special agent will return the compliment by ignoring you when he's calling the shots on God's turf.'

Jesus continued his theme. 'You know what? Some of you guys are actually going to see God's great outfit without even waiting to die.'

And now for something completely different . . .
(Mark 9:2-13)

Less than a week later, something fairly interesting happened. Jesus took Pete, James and his bro John for a wander up a hill. Just the four of them. And guess what, Jesus sort of totally transformed. One minute he was just Jesus. Next moment he was completely different – and bright as. His clothes were whiter than you'll ever get with Janola even. And wait, there's more! Old Moses and Elijah, who'd been quite dead for a few hundred years, there they were, nattering with Jesus.

'Hey, this is awesome!' Pete told Jesus as they stood there, with he and his mates being fairly gobsmacked by it all. Now, Pete was a man never afraid to speak without prior engagement of the brain, and one never short of a bright idea. So he added, 'I'm never short of a bright idea. Why don't we commemorate this fairly auspicious occasion by building a monument or three, one for you, one for Mo, and one for Elijah?'

Suddenly a cloud rolled up, covering them all and this voice came from the middle of it: 'This is my son, and a good lad at that, he really is all right! I reckon you'd do well to listen to him.'

Moments later, the cloud was gone, taking Mo and Elijah and Jesus' flash outfit with it. Back to ordinary. It was time to go down to the lower levels, and as they walked, Jesus told them straight: 'Say nothing about this to nobody, not till after God's number one bloke comes back from the dead.'

Pete and James and John told no one, but that didn't stop them chewing it over among themselves. What on earth did this 'getting out of the grave' stuff mean? As yet they didn't have a clue. Trying to get an angle on what had happened, they asked Jesus, 'Some of the religious teachers reckon Elijah comes first. What are they on about?'

Jesus told them, 'Yep, Elijah is first up, he sort of gets things under way. But hey, you'll recall that the good book reckons God's special agent is going to get some pretty rough treatment and then get booted out. That's pretty well exactly what they did to Elijah – you can read all about it.'

The kid with the evil force (Mark 9:14–29)

Down at the bottom of the hill were the rest of their mates, plus a whole bunch of others – and some of the religious types cross-examining them, or so it seemed. When they saw Jesus, he was a worthy alternative, so his fans mobbed him. 'What are you fellas arguing about?' Jesus asked them.

A bloke in the crowd saw his moment. 'Jesus!' he said. 'I've got me lad here, and he can't put two words together, he's got this force in him. It throws him down, makes him foam at the mouth, he's stiff as a poker. I asked these guys,' he added, gesturing to Jesus' mates (the ones who hadn't done the interesting hill climb), 'to sort it out, but they're useless as.'

'Why do I bother!' Jesus sighed in the direction of his useless mates. 'How many thousands of times do I have to say and do stuff to get it into your thick heads?' Turning to the man he said, 'Bring the kid to me.' The man brought the kid to Jesus. The evil force saw it was Jesus, and was less than pleased. It threw the kid into some sort of fit, rolling around on the ground and all. Jesus asked the dad, 'When did this stuff start?'

'When he was just a little ankle-biter,' Dad replied. 'Sometimes it's ended up with him getting burned on the barbie or half drowned in the lake. Please, please do something for us, boss. We're fairly desperate. Can you?'

'Can I *what*!' Jesus replied. 'Anyone who believes can do pretty well anything!'

'Count me in,' the desperate dad told him. 'I'll believe anything that's necessary to get me boy sorted – and I'd be glad if you'd give me a hand in so doing.'

This sort of stuff always had the potential to enlarge a crowd, and this time, sure as, Jesus could see more and more rolling up to catch the action. He quickly told the evil force, 'Hey get lost, totally so, and I'd advise you never ever to come within a million miles of this kid ever again.'

The force sort of yelled out, threw the kid all over the ground one last time, then disappeared, leaving the kid looking dead. 'He's dead!' the crowd helpfully observed.

Jesus was smarter than that. He took the kid by the hand and said, 'Up you get mate!' And up he got.

Jesus and his mates headed off inside for a break. 'Excuse me Jesus,' they asked him. 'We had a go at that but it didn't work for us. How come?'

'That sort of evil force is quite tough,' Jesus replied. 'You've gotta be praying, and praying well to do that kind.'

Jesus' mates get up themselves (Mark 9:30-37)

Time to move on again and find a bit of space away from the crowds. Jesus had a few things to point out to his mates. 'God's number one bloke is going to get narked on. They're going to take him out – but you know what? Three days later he'll be back in town.' His mates didn't have a clue what he was on about – nor did they have the guts to tell him so.

They wandered further down the road and entered another town. Once inside the house out of the sun, Jesus asked them, 'You had plenty to say among yourselves as we strolled. Penny for your thoughts, eh?' Now, this was rather embarrassing, because as they'd talked they'd sort of been competing to see who could be more up themselves than the others. The sort of conversation you'd certainly not be inclined to tell the boss about. Jesus, of course, could see right through them. 'I can see right through you,' he told them. 'If you want to be kingpin, then you've actually got to, like, work the hardest. You've got to look out for everyone else first – for real.'

To further emphasise his point, Jesus picked up a passing kid and gave him a hug. 'You know what? If you care about kids and treat them good, it means you care about me. And there's more – if you care about me, you care about God who sent me. And that's gotta be pretty cool.'

Some competitors are doing stuff (Mark 9:38-41)

'Hey boss,' said John, sort of taking a bit of a detour in the conversation, 'we saw some guy we didn't know who was doing your sort of stuff with evil forces in people. He was attributing it to you even! Naturally, him not being a member of our team and all, we told him to quit. Good, eh?'

'Bad call, John,' Jesus told him. 'If anybody reckons they're doing something in my name, they can't very well be slagging me off next moment, eh? If anybody's not against me, he's one of us. Simple. Mate, if you so much as give someone a glass of H_2O because I've inspired you, you'll do all right.'

Don't do stupid things (Mark 9:42-50)

Jesus continued: 'I'm going to warn you guys – if any one of you does anything, *anything* to make it hard for one of these kids who are following me, man, it's going to be bad for you. You'll find it would have been better if your feet had been set in concrete and you got yourself tossed off the boat for a swim. Listen, if your hands or feet are liable to cause you to do stupid things, then you'd be better to have them surgically removed and wander around armless and legless than find yourselves ending up in a place that's hot as hell.'

Warming to his subject, Jesus added, 'Same goes for your eyes. If you're looking at too much rubbish which is doing you no good, poke 'em out! Similar reasoning. You've got to agree that it's smarter to turn up in heaven visually impaired than with 20/20 vision in the other place – which, by the way, is thoroughly unrecommended, and is more than stink.'

Jesus concluded the subject by telling them, 'Listen, everybody's gotta get the bad bits trimmed off. It's a worthwhile process even though it can be fairly painful at times. Putting it another way, a little bit of salt does wonders to a meal, but if it's thoroughly past its use-by date, then its value is stuff all. It's a good idea to keep yourselves like a pinch of real good salt. And while you're about it, see if you can avoid scrapping among yourselves too.'

Divorce is a stupid idea (Mark 10:1-12)

Jesus moved off, crossed the river, and headed to a new patch. As per usual, the crowds weren't slow to catch up with his where-abouts, his reputation making him such an interesting guy to be around and all. And as per usual, he had plenty of wise stuff to say, which they lapped right up.

Also as per usual, some religious guys turned up. 'What's your views on a bloke getting a divorce?' they asked him.

Jesus answered their question with one of his own. 'What did old Moses have to say on the subject?'

'That's easy,' they replied. 'Old Moses said we could just give her the documents and tell her she was out of here.'

'You know what?' Jesus asked. 'It's because you're such a miserable pack of sods that Moses made it easy for you to get a divorce. That wasn't how God intended it way back at the beginning, no sir. The original idea was once you get married, you're a unit together. For keeps. If God has worked it out like that, then it's particularly stupid to try and split up a marriage.'

Once they got home for the day, Jesus' mates raised the subject again. 'It's quite straightforward, really,' he said. 'If anyone divorces their bloke or their sheila so as they can head out and marry someone else, that's just a straight no-no. Against the rules, end of story.'

Jesus and kids (Mark 10:13-16)

One day, people were bringing their kids to Jesus because they knew he had a nice way with them and the kids liked him. Jesus' mates, however, felt Jesus should be in a kid-free zone. They weren't going to have mere youngsters disrupting the show. Jesus was rather hacked off with their attitude. 'I'm hacked off with your attitude,' he told his mates. 'Let the wee tykes come to me – believe it or not, kids like these are going to be right at the heart of God's great outfit.'

With that, Jesus picked up one of the kids, then gave them all a blessing. Which they liked, that's for sure.

The bloke who was loaded (Mark 10:17-31)

Jesus was about to head off with his mates when this bloke ran up to him. 'Gidday,' he said to Jesus. 'You're a good bloke. Tell me, what do I have to do to get a sort of life membership of your great outfit?'

'Why do you call me "good"?' Jesus asked the guy. 'You know what? The only one who deserves to be called "good" is God. Anyhow, you know the rules: no killing, no knocking around with someone else's woman, no nicking what ain't yours, don't tell no lies, don't rip off the taxman and respect your olds.'

'Listen mate,' said the bloke, 'I've done – or not done, as appropriate – all of the above, since I was a kid.'

Jesus looked at the bloke and gave him a hearty slap on the back. 'You're my sort of type,' he told him. 'There's just one more thing I want then.'

'Yeah?' asked the guy, very interested. 'What's that?'

'Quite simple,' Jesus told him. 'All you've got to do is go and sell your stuff and give the proceeds to the poor. That's all.'

'Um, which stuff in particular did you have in mind?' the bloke asked him.

'Everything,' Jesus replied. 'Just do it! Then, and only then, will you have things correctly organised for the hereafter. When you've liquidated *everything*, given away every last cent to the poor, then you can come and join up with me and the lads.' Now, this bloke was loaded like you wouldn't believe. And when Jesus said that to him his face fell – and a fairly long fall it was too – and he took off down the road.

Jesus looked around and said to his mates, 'How hard it is for those who are loaded to count when the chips are down.' This took them somewhat by surprise (they probably had a few bucks stashed away themselves). 'Guys, it's a good deal easier to get a mob of sheep to head exactly where you want them without dogs or anything than it is for a rich bloke to be part of God's great outfit.'

'Well I never!' said his mates. 'Doesn't really give anyone a monkey's chance, eh?'

'Generally speaking, you're right,' Jesus replied. 'Fact is, from a human perspective, not a chance. But with God, well, that's a different story. God can do anything, *anything*!'

Pete turned to Jesus and said, 'Well, us guys have left everything behind to follow you. Good, eh?'

'You know what?' Jesus told them. 'Anyone who's keen enough to put first all the stuff I've been telling you about – and put that as a higher-priority ranking than their olds, their bros and sisters and investments – well, they're going to do all right. They'll get a stack of stuff and a much bigger whanau too. But more hassles, I should add. Plus full membership of God's great outfit. Those who get things out of perspective now and just live for the present, well, they're going to end up at the bottom of the heap. And vice versa.'

Jesus still sees death down the track
(Mark 10:32-34)

By now they were heading down the road to the big city, Jerusalem. His mates were straggling further behind, totally blown away by all of that. Even the groupies were a tad worried. Jesus took his twelve close mates aside. 'As you will have observed,' he told them, 'this particular road heads to Jerusalem. And this is what's going to happen. Like I said, God's special agent is going to get narked on to the religious heavies. They're going to say, "Curtains for you, mate!" and hand him over to the military occupiers. Those guys will beat him senseless, then take him out. And three days later he'll be back in town.'

James and John get up themselves
(Mark 10:35-45)

James and John (the two Zeb boys) snuck up to Jesus when the others weren't noticing. 'Bit of a request,' they said to him, 'which we hope you won't mind organising for us.'

'And that is?' Jesus replied.

'Quite straightforward, really. When the show is over and you're finally in your rightful place as kingpin, we'd be rather chuffed if one of us can sit on your right, the other on your left. OK by you?'

'You've gotta be joking!' Jesus told them. 'Have you any idea at all just what you're on about? Have you the faintest idea of all the grief and suffering which is looking me square in the eye?'

'Yep, for sure!' James and John replied. (Yeah, right!)

'Little do you know the truth of what you're saying, cos yep, you are going to come to grief and big-time too. But as to handing out places in the corporate box, that task isn't on my horizon. And anyhow, those who are already lined up for those spots, they're the ones who'll get them.'

It wasn't long before the other guys heard what they'd been on about. Talk about stuff hitting the fan – they were distinctly less than impressed with James and John getting so up themselves. Jesus, spotting a fisticuffs in the making, called them all over.

'Listen boys!' he instructed them. 'In all probability you will have noticed that the politicians and their departmental lackeys like sticking it to the masses. But that's not how it is to be. Like I said last week, if you want to be kingpin, then you've actually got to be the most ordinary of the lot. You've got to lick the boots of everyone else. Even God's special agent didn't come here to live in the lap of luxury, but rather to do stuff for others. And he came prepared to give up his life in favour of everyone else, which you've got to see is a fairly significant position to take.'

Bart gets a new look (Mark 10:46-52)

After a bit of transit time in this place called Jericho, Jesus and his mates (followed by the regular swag of hangers-on) hit the road. On the edge of town, just by the open-road sign, was this visually impaired guy by the name of Bart. When he heard that it was Jesus passing by, he yelled out, 'Hey Jesus, I need a bit of a hand here!'

'Shut up you!' was the general view of the crowd – and they expressed it without hesitation. That didn't deter old Bart, not a chance of that. He shouted louder still, 'Jesus – help me out, please!'

Jesus heard him and stopped. 'Bring him here, eh,' he said. So the crowd changed their tune. 'Good news mate,' they told him. 'Jesus wants to see you.' So he threw off his jacket and went charging over to where Jesus was.

'Kia ora,' Jesus said to him. 'What can I do for you, mate?'

'Guess what?' Bart replied. 'I'd like to see.'

'Done!' said Jesus. 'Cos of that little bit of faith you showed, you're right as rain.' Just as Jesus had said, the guy could see – immediately. So he joined in with the crowd following Jesus.

Chapter 6

STUFF IN JERUSALEM

The big parade (Mark 11:1-11)

The roadshow was getting closer to Jerusalem, and they passed a couple of towns near this hill with lots of olives growing on it. Jesus gave a job to a couple of his mates. 'Listen guys,' he told them. 'I'd like you to drop in on that village down there, and you'll find a young donkey parked outside the pub. Pick it up for me, would you? If anyone spots you in the act, tell them, "No worries, the boss sent us over for the beast, and he'll have it back to you in no time."'

So the two blokes basically did just that. Down the road at the next village, the donkey was there. They untied it and the owner spotted them in the act. They told him, 'No worries, the boss sent us over for the beast, and he'll have it back to you in no time.' Just like that.

They brought the donkey back to where Jesus was, stuck their jackets on it because the seat was a bit lumpy, and Jesus got on. As he rode down the road people planted their jackets on it, being the way they showed their respect. They also provided some branches as a sort of red-carpet treatment. People all over the show were enthusiastically yelling out, 'Hey man, fantastic! Cheers, ra-ra, hey cool, you're the one for us!' and stuff like that.

Jesus made it into town and went to the temple there. He took a quick look-see all around, but what with it being a bit late in the day, decided to duck off home with his mates to their regular stopping-off point in that particular locale.

The tree that didn't give a fig (Mark 11:12-14)

On their way back into the city next morning, Jesus noticed this leafy fig tree. Wandering over to pick a few for a feed, he discovered to his surprise that the tree was entirely fig-less. He figured that was a bit useless, even though in fact it wasn't quite time for the fruit anyhow. Jesus spoke to the tree – for real: 'Hey you, it's curtains for you in the production department. I wouldn't give a fig for your future.' Jesus' mates overheard this little one-sided conversation.

The rip-off artists at the temple (Mark 11:15-19)

Anyhow, they got back into Jerusalem, and Jesus went straight to the temple where there were stacks of traders buying and selling practically anything that moved. 'You can all take a running jump!' he told them in no uncertain terms and knocked over the cashiers' tables, and all the shelves of those selling birds. 'The good book says this has got to be a place for praying,' he said, 'but you're just a pack of crooks.'

The religious bosses got wind of what he'd done and they were distinctly unimpressed. They reckoned he had to be done in – they were feeling somewhat threatened by him because everybody was just soaking up all he had to say. Come evening time, Jesus and his mates got right out of there.

The fig tree that wasn't (Mark 11:20-26)

Next morning, they happened to pass the aforementioned fig

tree. Dead as, it was an ex-tree for sure. 'Hey Jesus', said Pete. 'The tree you had a go at, well, it's karked it.'

'You've got to have faith in God, simple as that,' Jesus told them. 'You know what? It's like when you've got such faith, then you can tell a mountain to take a running jump into the sea. If you really believe it, it will (so to speak). The point is, seriously now, if you ask God for genuine stuff and believe it's right, then you'll get it.

'An important thing to keep in mind when you're doing your praying is that if you hold a grudge against some other bloke, let it go, forgive him! If you're prepared to do that, then God up top can forgive you *your* stuff-ups. However, if you can't be bothered forgiving someone, then I'm afraid to say God won't be bothered forgiving you either.'

Who do you think you are? (Mark 11:27-33)

Back at the temple, Jesus was strolling through the grounds when some of the religious leaders came up to him. 'Just who the blazes do you think you are, doing all this stuff?' they asked him. 'Who exactly *is* your boss?'

Jesus turned it straight back on them. 'I've got a question for you – answer it, then I'll answer yours. That guy John who used to dunk people in the creek – where did *he* get that from? Was it just *his* clever idea, or was God actually behind that lot?'

'We're screwed,' they said among themselves. 'If we say it's from God then he'll say we're dorks for not believing it. But if we say it was just John being up himself, we'll be in trouble because the crowds thought John was a great bloke.' What to do? A bit of wiggling seemed to be in order. 'Sorry Jesus, we can't answer that one,' they replied.

'Fair enough,' said Jesus. 'Quits. I won't answer yours either.'

Hear the one about the crook tenants?
(Mark 12:1-12)

Jesus told them a few fairly good stories. Like this one:

'A bloke planted a vineyard. He fenced it all around, built some processing facilities and a security post. Then he leased it out and took off for a tour of some distant spot. Come harvest time he sent one of the lads to collect his cut from the harvest as per the contract. But you know what? The tenants grabbed him by the ear, gave him a good hiding and sent him packing. So the owner sent another of his workers. For his trouble he got thoroughly whacked on the head and generally treated disrespectfully. You wouldn't have wanted to be number three on the list – he just got killed for giving it a go. The boss kept sending people, and they kept getting killed or nearly so. By this time he was running out of people to send. Except his own boy, a good lad he was too. So Dad sent him to do his bit. "Surely they will respect him," Dad said. But no, afraid not. "If we kill him, the place is ours!" they said enthusiastically. So kill him they did, and yet another one bit the dust. What would the owner do now? He'd head straight over and beat them within an inch of their lives – then do that final inch for good measure, wouldn't he?'

Jesus continued. 'The good book says something about that – a bunch of builders rejected what turned out to be the most significant part of the whole shooting box! God's got it sussed, and it's pretty good, eh?'

The religious authorities just knew he was getting at them, so they tried to get him booked on some charge – anything would do. The problem was the ordinary people, who were just about eating out of Jesus' hand. Right now wasn't the best time to pick a fight with that lot around. So they let him be, and Jesus scarpered.

Do you have to pay tax? (Mark 12:13-17)

Later on, these same guys sent some of their mates to try and catch Jesus out. 'Hey man,' they said to him, casual like. 'You're a good and honest sort of bloke, we know that for sure. You don't lose your cool under pressure, you're good at knowing God's perspective on stuff. We've got a particularly interesting question for you. Should we keep paying extortionist taxes to the occupying government or tell them to get stuffed?'

Jesus was no fool, and he could see right through those guys. 'I can see right through you,' he told them. 'Show me a dollar.' They showed him a dollar. 'All right, whose mug is on the coin?'

'Our wonderful leader's,' they replied.

'Simple, then,' said Jesus. 'Give the government what you're supposed to give the government, and give God what you're supposed to give God.' Wow, they couldn't fault that for an answer. You could have knocked them down with a feather.

The serial widow (Mark 12:18–27)

Next up, another bunch of religious leaders bowled along, and this particular lot reckoned once you karked it, it was curtains, no hereafter. 'Dude,' they started respectfully. 'Old Moses reckoned that if a bloke dies leaving a wife but no littlies, then his bro ought to marry the poor old widow and provide her with some kids. Now, look at this hypothetical scenario. There were seven bros. The first died kid-less. So his first brother married the widow, but he too up and died minus sprogs. So his next bro took up the responsibility, but he met the same fate, and again no kids. This happened several more times until they ran out of brothers. And the woman was probably worn out with the seven of them, so she died. Our question – and this is the key to it all – in the great hereafter, which particular bloke is her husband?'

Jesus sighed. 'You guys have lost the plot. For one thing, you don't know the good book too well. For another, you just don't know how God's got it all organised in the hereafter. The point is, when this era is done for, so is getting married and having kids. In that respect you'll end up like a pack of angels. As for what happens to the dead ones when time finishes, don't you ever read old Moses' book properly? In that particular volume, when God spoke to Moses around the time of that burning bush episode, he told him, "I am the God of Abraham and his kids and grandkids etc." Guys, he's God of the *living*, not of the dead! You really are way off beam.'

Keys to successful living (Mark 12:28-34)

One of the theological types was eavesdropping on all of this with a fair degree of interest. 'Smart answer that,' he said to himself, and decided to ask Jesus a question of his own: 'Of all the rules and things we're supposed to live by, which particular one do you reckon is the tops?'

Jesus replied, 'It's the one that goes: "Listen everybody! God is God and is the boss. You've got to love God with everything in you – every last part of you." And the next in importance is this one: "Watch out for your mates' interests, treat them as good as you." There's nothing anywhere that beats those two.'

'Fair enough,' the guy told him. 'You're spot on with that – there's just one God and that's it. And the bit about loving God full on, that's good too. And the stuff about watching out for your mates – you've got it there too. That's what all God's rules come down to in the end.'

Jesus realised that he was one sensible bloke. 'You're well on the right track, mate,' he told him. Everyone around could see that Jesus was smart as, so no one else had the guts to try him out on any more smart-aleck questions.

Religious leaders (Mark 12:35-40)

Jesus was yakking to the people around the temple and he asked them, 'How come the religious leaders say God's number one bloke that they're all hanging out for is going to be a descendant of old King David from yonks back? Because, you see, old David

seemed fairly awed by whoever would be this special bloke –
seems a bit odd him talking like that if he was going to end up
as his umpteenth great-grandson, wouldn't you say?' The crowd
thought Jesus was pretty smart with that one.

Jesus carried on talking with the crowd. 'Watch out for the
Bible-bashers,' he warned them. 'They love poncing around in
their fancy outfits, having people bowing and scraping. They're
so up themselves, they sit at the top table at any function they
can. Watch them – they act as if they're better than anyone, but
they'll rip you off quick as look at you. I tell you, they'll get
what's coming to them.'

The little old lady with twenty cents (Mark 12:41–44)

Jesus sat himself down within eyeshot of the collection plate near
the door of the temple one day. People from all over were
coming and going and sticking in their money. Jesus could see
the rich guys making their contributions in a way so people
could see just how generous they were. Then a little old lady
snuck up and surreptitiously dropped a mere twenty cents into
the plate – worth stuff all then as now. Jesus called his mates over
and said, 'See that old dear and the infinitesimal bit she stuck in
the plate? You know what? She's in fact forked out substantially
more than all those rich jokers. In case you think I'm losing my
marbles, what I mean is this: those other guys we were watching
are totally loaded. So the few bucks they threw in aren't even a
drop in the bucket as far as their net worth goes. But her – she
put in all the cash she had, every last cent, she did. Think on that.'
They did.

Jesus warns of tough times ahead (Mark 13:1–37)

As they wandered out of the temple, one of his mates said to
him, 'Hey mate, look at those big-mama stones they've used in
the construction. Fancy, eh?'

'You know what?' Jesus replied. 'These posh edifices, they're all going to, like, disappear, and there'll be diddly squat left.' He and his mates sat down on a nearby park bench on the hill, and Pete, James and John thought this an opportune time to put a question to him on the quiet.

'Jesus,' they asked, 'just when is this sort of stuff you're talking about going to happen? And how the blazes will we know that it's all about to hit the fan?'

'Take care that no one takes you for a ride,' Jesus told them. 'You see, all sorts are going to turn up in town and claim to be me. And there's the usual suckers who'll believe them. There'll be the usual wars and threats, but don't get your knickers in a twist. I'm afraid to say, those sorts will always be around – but eventually we'll still call it quits. Meantime, you'll have invasions and coups and stuff. Along with that will be the odd earthquake here and there, famines and all – but these won't be a patch on what's coming, no sir! So listen guys, take good care, OK? Cos you know what? The toughs are going to give you a real hard time. Yep, they're going to beat the living daylights out of you – and sometimes it's even going to happen in church! You'll be appearing, of course, down at the district court. You'll be giving an account of yourselves – and of me too, you see. We've gotta get the story out, OK?

'Here's a tip for you: when you get picked up and taken to court, don't get yourself steamed up about what to say. Just say stuff right off the top of your head – believe it or not, God's Spirit will stick some useful words in your mouth at just the right time. Good, eh?

'Things are going to get a bit rich, actually. You won't even be able to trust your bro not to sell you down the line. Or your old man. Not even your kids. I'm sorry to say, some of them are going to see to it that their olds get strung up – which isn't particularly nice, really. Because you're one of my mates, every-one will be in a despising mood as far as you're concerned. But if you hang on in there mate, you'll do all right.

'One day, however, you're going to see something incredibly awful and totally scary. Now, when that happens, boy, you'd better get outta the place. Take to the hills – and quick-like. Don't so much as go and collect your sipper bottle or credit card – nothing! I tell you, it's going to be quite tough if you're pregnant or you've got nippers. And it's not a bad idea if you pray that this stuff won't happen in winter, because it's going to be real, *real* tough – like nothing you could ever imagine. But here's a bit of good news: God's going to cut this stuff shorter than it might have been. Otherwise it would be curtains for everyone – *everyone*! For God's mates, he's made it shorter. Just as well, eh?

'From time to time blokes are going to say to you, "Hey, guess what? Here comes God's special bloke." Load of cobblers, I'm telling you. The place will be crawling with these so-called God-agents – they'll be doing all sorts of fancy stuff to fool you, if they can. But that's why I've told you all this stuff, so that you can keep your eyes wide open. And there's more. After all of the aforementioned, the sun is going to be a bit short in the light and warmth departments, and even the moon will take a sabbatical. As for the stars and stuff, they'll be having some off days too. But then God's number one bloke will arrive, and it will be sort of "Wow!" All God's lower-level agents will be on collecting duty, picking up God's genuine mates from hither and yon, they will – every last one.

'Hey guys, cast your minds back to fig trees and stuff – I'm referring to them in general rather than that particular fig tree that became an ex-fig tree. Anyhow, you'd do well to take a tip or two from that particular species. If you watch it starting to bud and produce leaves and stuff, you can bet your bottom dollar that summer is just around the corner. Well, it's exactly the same with what I've been telling you – when all that stuff happens, you'll know that the future has turned up right on your doorstep. I'd recommend that you take this fairly seriously – cos it's actually going to happen bang in front of your very eyes before your number's called.

'I'm telling you for real, this whole shooting box is going to vaporise some time, but the stuff I'm telling you, it's sure as eggs – well, surer in fact. As for the actual time and date, there's nobody, not a soul, who has a note of the timetable. Nobody nowhere, not even me! Just one exception – God knows it. Nobody else. Got it? So watch yourselves, you blokes. You just never know when this action is going to begin. It's sort of like this bloke is going away for a lengthy break. He puts a house-sitter into his pad to keep an eye on things and keep the show in good order. Now, it's a fairly good idea for the bloke in that house-sitting position to keep the house in good shape, you'd think. Cos you just never know when the boss might turn up. You don't want to get caught out with the place half trashed at whatever time of day or night, eh?'

Jesus concluded: 'Well, to sum up what I've been telling you, keep your big ugly eyes open, OK?'

Chapter 7

GOOD FRIDAY, EASTER AND BEYOND

Jesus and the fancy fragrance (Mark 14:1–9)

Well, Easter time was just about to happen (it wasn't called
Easter back then – they actually called it Passover). Anyhow, the
God squad thought it a potentially good time to catch Jesus and
do him in, and so they were trying to suss out some sneaky way
of doing just that.

'A useful tip,' some of them were saying, 'is that it wouldn't
be the smartest thing to do it while people are in party mode.
The crowd would have your guts for garters, they would.'

Jesus, meantime, was up the road at a mate's place (another
of the Simons, actually, but this one was not so good in the skin
department cos bits kept dropping off him). Well, this woman
turned up with a bottle of perfume that was fairly pricey, to say
the least. She cracked it open and then – yes – poured it on Jesus'
head. The lot of it! Some of the bunch of people there were
distinctly unimpressed with that. 'What a complete and utter

waste of such a fancy fragrance,' they moaned. 'That particular brand is priced out of this world – it's worth more than thirty grand a bottle! It would have been a bit smarter, actually, to have sold it off and used the proceeds to help out a few of the down-and-out-ers, eh?' they went on, warming to their theme. 'You're a loser!' they told her.

'Get lost!' Jesus told them. 'Why are you giving her heaps? She's done a fairly significant thing as far as I'm concerned. Your bit about the down-and-out-ers – they're always around, for sure. And, of course, you've got the opportunity to do something decent for the poor whenever it takes your fancy. But me, who she did this for, well, it so happens that I won't be hanging around these parts forever. You probably don't realise it, but what she's done is real special, eh – in fact, it's preparing me in advance for my pending burial following my pending demise.

'You know what?' Jesus continued. 'What has just happened is going to be told about for time immemorial – which you've got to admit, is a fairly long time. Whenever people get the good oil that I've been on about, this particular incident will be part of the story.'

Jude does a deal (Mark 14:10–11)

One of Jesus' mates was this bloke called Judas, who was a part-time accountant. He saw a useful income opportunity, so he went to the religious leaders and offered to give them the lowdown on where Jesus was hanging out and how they could get their hands on him. Well, the God squad thought this a pretty good idea and offered some significant financial incentives. This psyched Jude up no end, and he decided to suss out the right moment as quick as, so he could get his hands on the dosh.

Jesus' final feed (Mark 14:12–31)

As already noted, this was one of the times of the year when the people in those days used to have a bit of a celebration party. So they asked Jesus, 'How do you reckon we should celebrate this year?'

Jesus replied, 'See that guy over there? Follow him down to the local and book out a function room, which ought to be free that night, according to my reckoning. Tell him the boss is wanting to put on his Passover party there with his mates.'

Sure as eggs, he was right, so they booked it and got ready for the party.

Jesus and his mates turned up that evening and got stuck into the food. While they were eating, Jesus said, 'You know what? One of you lot's going to turn me in to the cops.'

This sort of caused them to choke on their meal. 'Well, it ain't me,' each of them said with a fair degree of certainty.

'It's one of you, for sure,' said Jesus. 'In fact, whoever stuck his bread into the dip at the same time as I did, he's the one. And I'll say this: it would be a darn sight better for that bloke if his mother hadn't been fertile round that particular time.'

As you can imagine, that did put a bit of a dampener on the party. As they continued eating, Jesus picked up a piece of pita bread. He thanked God for it, then passed bits of it round to the guys sitting there. 'This,' he said, 'stands for my body.'

Jesus then picked up the wine bottle, poured a glass, again thanked God, and handed it around for them all to have a swig. 'This wine,' he told them, 'it stands for my blood – it's God's promise, and my blood is going to be poured out for stacks of people. And you know what? I'll not be imbibing another drop of the grape till I enjoy a glass of it when God's great outfit comes.'

They sang a song which was one of their favourites, then went out and up the hill. As they were walking along, Jesus said, 'You know what? You blokes are all going to give me the slip.'

Pete said, 'Well, *those* guys might, but you can count on me, boss.'

Jesus replied, 'You know what? Before the rooster goes off in the morning, three times you'll have said you ain't one of my mates.'

'No way!' said Pete, digging his toes in. 'I'd rather get strung up with you than give you the cold shoulder.'

'Too right mate, same here!' chorused the others.

At Gethsemane Park (Mark 14:32–42)

They walked on till they arrived at this park called Gethsemane. Jesus said to his mates, 'You can stop here and do a bit of praying, OK?' He walked on further himself, taking Pete, James and John with him. By now he was getting quite stewed up about things.

'This whole thing's getting a bit much for me,' he said. 'You three stay here, and I'll go on a bit further. He staggered on a bit, then collapsed to the ground. 'For goodness' sake, God,' he said, 'can't you *please* get me out of this? But if you don't see yourself doing that, well, I guess I'll have to stick with it.'

He went back to his mates and, believe it or not, they were out to it. 'Hey Pete!' he said. 'Can't you keep your eyes open for even one circuit of the hour hand? Get yourself together mate, I need your support. Yes, I know you care about me Pete, but if you don't watch out you'll end up in trouble.'

Jesus went off and poured out his heart to God again, same as last time. When he came back, yep, dead to the world they were yet again. They woke up and felt more than a bit stink – they knew this was a huge thing eating away at Jesus, and they knew they were letting the side down big-time too. Jesus took off once again, came back and, exactly the same as before, they were packing zzzs. Jesus really gave them what for this time: 'For crying out loud, you guys are just sleeping your lives away. Get up! The action is about to start.'

Jesus gets nabbed (Mark 14:43–52)

Right as he said it, Jude came round the corner. With him was a bunch of thugs hired by the religious types, and these guys were armed to the eyeballs. Jude had told them in advance how they could identify Jesus: 'I'll give him a hearty slap on the back and say, "How's it going, mate?"'

Jude did just that. 'How's it going, mate?' he greeted Jesus as he gave him a big friendly slap on the back. Quick as, the toughs grabbed Jesus. One of Jesus' mates was less than impressed with that. He whipped out a knife and had a piece of one of the religious team – in fact, he removed part of the bloke's hearing equipment.

Jesus said to the mob, 'What do you take me for, with all that firepower? Do you think I'm some kind of terrorist? You've seen me down there by the temple every day, and you didn't pick me up then, so what goes? What you're doing is going to more than get you in the history books, I tell you.'

By this time Jesus' mates had got the wind up them good and proper, so they took off. One bloke who sort of knew him a bit was following nearby, and the thugs grabbed him. He was just wearing a pair of shorts, actually, and they ripped as he struggled. He took to the wind starkers, leaving them holding his boxers.

The kangaroo court begins (Mark 14:53–65)

The mob took Jesus downtown where the main God squad was, and all the religious heavies got together to take a look because this was big-time. Pete went downtown too to see what was going to happen, and he mingled with the security guys at the bar. The legal types were yakking among themselves to see what sort of charges they could trump up to finish Jesus off, but they were a bit short of hard data. No worries, they got a few of the rent-a-crowd mob to make up some likely-sounding stories, but the stories didn't match up, which was just a tad embarrassing.

The CEO from the religious department turned to Jesus: 'Listen mate, what have you got to say for yourself? What's your particular take on what those guys are alleging?'

Jesus said nix.

The CEO had another go: 'Are you God's number one bloke?'

'You've got it,' Jesus told him. 'And one of these days you'll see that particular character sitting right next to God up in the clouds.'

The religious chief was distinctly unhappy with that, and ripped his clothes, it being a fairly common kind of protest action back then. 'I reckon we've heard more than enough!' he shouted. 'You've heard the outrageous stuff he's saying. Whaddaya say?' he asked the assembled mob.

'String him up!' everyone energetically replied. Some of them began spitting straight in his eye. They tied a rag around his eyes so he couldn't see, then proceeded to beat him up. 'OK, smart guy,' they challenged him. 'If you're so clever, name the guys who hit you!' Security took their cue and beat him good and hard too.

Pete tells a few lies (Mark 14:66–72)

Pete, meantime, was still down at the bar, and one of the staff there noticed him. 'Hey you,' she said. 'You're a mate of that bloke Jesus!'

'Don't be so stupid!' Pete replied. 'Never seen him before.' All the same, he headed for the door to get out of a potentially awkward situation. But he didn't get far enough. The same sheila saw him again out there.

'Hey guys,' she said. 'That bloke is one of Jesus' mates. I recognise him!'

'Get lost!' Pete told her. 'You don't know what you're talking about.'

Rather stupidly in terms of his own well-being, Pete still hung about. A few of the others nearabouts also noticed that he seemed the same sort of type who used to hang around with Jesus. 'Come on man, you *are* one of his gang. It's clear as,' they said.

As if to prove he wasn't, Pete let out a string of four-letter words. 'I tell you, I wouldn't have the faintest what you're on about. He *ain't* a mate of mine. Finito!'

Just then a distant rooster did its early-morning thing. Suddenly Pete remembered what Jesus had said not a few hours ago: 'Before the rooster goes off in the morning, three times you will have said you ain't one of my mates.' That really broke Pete up, and he realised what a right sod he really was.

The kangaroo court continues (Mark 15:1-20)

Next day, well before the sun appeared over the horizon, the religious leaders and all their legal eagles and councils reached their foregone conclusion. They handcuffed Jesus and took him down to the local governor, a bloke by the name of Pilate.

'Hey you!' Pilate said to Jesus. 'Tell me, are you the King of the Jews?'

'You said it,' Jesus replied.

At this point the religious leaders laid out their charges – covering pretty well any and everything. Pilate then said to Jesus, 'Well mate, they've said a fair few derogatory things about you and what you've been up to. It would be a fairly useful idea for you to offer a view on it all, eh?'

Jesus said absolutely nothing, zilch. Pilate couldn't believe his eyes – or his ears.

Back in those days, every Easter weekend they used to let a guy out of jail as a sort of goodwill gesture. It so happened there was this guy Barabbas who'd been locked up for a goodly stretch for doing terrorist stuff. Well, the crowd came to Pilate and asked him to do the usual thing – let someone out early.

'Presumably this guy Jesus would be the guy who I should let out?' Pilate asked them, knowing that the religious types had actually set him up a bit because they were feeling a touch jealous of all Jesus' popularity. The religious guys, however, weren't so easily taken for a ride. They conned the crowd into asking for, would you believe, Barabbas to get parole instead.

'What about this bloke Jesus, then?' he asked them.

'String him up!' they replied energetically.

'What the hell for?' Pilate asked them. 'What's his crime?'

The crowd, by now beyond intelligent reason, ignored Pilate's common-sense question. 'String him up!' they yelled even more energetically.

This left Pilate in a bit of a spot. Wanting to keep in good with the crowd, he told Barabbas he was commuting his sentence and let him go. As for Jesus, Pilate got security to beat him up, then sent him off to be done in. The cops took Jesus off to this fancy palace and got the complete bunch of on-duty officers together. They stuck him in some flash clothes, made a sort of crown out of gorse and stuck it on his head. 'Wow sir, you're the fancy-pants king, eh?' they mocked him.

Then they whacked him some more, added some spit to the insults, and pretended to treat him like a real bigwig. Then it was time to move on to the next phase, taking him out for good, which was going to involve nailing him to a post.

Jesus is assassinated (Mark 15:21–41)

As they went off down the road, this bloke called Simon was passing through town, so the cops grabbed him and made him carry the big post. Eventually they got to this morbid place called 'The Skull' up on a hill. They offered him a beer mixed with a bit of perfumed medicinal, but Jesus wasn't having any of it. Then they grabbed him and nailed him to the big post, with his arms stuck out on the crossbar. By this time it was nine o'clock, and they now gambled off his clothes among themselves. To make it clear what Jesus was up for, they stuck up a notice saying 'The King of the Jews'. On either side of him were a couple of crooks that they strung up at the same time, same method.

'*Now* who's the smart guy?' some of the passers-by yelled at him. 'You reckoned you could knock over the temple and have it up again in three days. That being the case, getting down from that post should be a breeze. Why don't you, then?'

The religious lot put in their two cents' worth. 'He did *such* a fine job in helping others out of a spot. But when it's *him* up the creek without a paddle, he doesn't seem to be able to do stuff all.' In a mocking tone, they added, 'Come on you, you're the clever-clogs King of the Jews, do one of your specials and get down off that post, and we'll be your mates till the cows come home!' The crooks on the adjacent posts also had a go at him.

At lunchtime the whole place got incredibly dark – and it stayed like that till afternoon teatime. Around then, Jesus called out, 'Hey God, why have you left me in the lurch?'

Some of the onlookers who may have been a bit hard of hearing thought he was calling out for Elijah, a good bloke from way back who of course was long gone. One guy grabbed a sponge, soaked it in beer and offered it to him. 'Hey mate,' he mocked, 'let's see if your pal Elijah turns up to get you out of this.'

Right then, Jesus let out a loud cry and he was done for. At exactly that time, down at the temple, the curtain up the front tore itself in half, starting from the top and right down to the bottom. The head of security was standing in front of Jesus on the post. When he heard his death cry, he said, 'Wow, that guy really *was* God's special bloke!'

Some of Jesus' female friends were watching from a bit further out, including a couple of Marys and Sal. These women used to be part of Jesus' travelling roadshow and in charge of catering and stuff. There were a fair few other women there too – they'd come out in solidarity with Jesus.

A borrowed grave (Mark 15:42–47)

As evening got close, this guy called Joe, one of the local leaders, fronted up to Pilate and asked him if he could take Jesus' body. This caught Pilate somewhat by surprise. 'Don't tell me he's dead *already*?' asked Pilate. He called the head of security to get confirmation.

'Sure thing,' security told Pilate. This being the case, Pilate told Joe that he could take Jesus' body. Joe went down to the fabric shop, bought some high-quality linen, carefully wrapped Jesus in it, then took him down to the cemetery. He put Jesus in a grave carved out of the hillside, then he stuck this big rock across the entrance. The two Marys watched all this from a safe distance.

Jesus stops being dead (Mark 16:1-8)

The two Marys and Sal went and got some special embalming stuff for Jesus' body. Next morning, crack of dawn, they headed down towards the cemetery. 'Who's going to remove that humungous rock from in front of his grave?' they asked each other on the way. But when they got there, they discovered to their surprise that this particular activity was going to be superfluous – it was done already. So they went right into the grave itself, and were a bit knocked back to find this bloke sitting there wearing all white gear.

'Don't get your knickers in a knot!' he told them. 'More than likely I reckon you're looking for Jesus, right? The bloke who got strung up? Well, guess what, he's up! He's alive! Fantastic news, eh? Here, cast your eyes in this direction and you'll see where he was and now ain't.'

The white-clad guy continued: 'Don't just hang around here, though. Go and see his mates – Pete in particular – and tell them that Jesus has headed off down to the beach. For real, you'll find him down there just like he told you!'

Now the Marys were a bit unsure about all of this – fairly scared in fact. So they took to their heels out of the graveyard and said nix to nobody, because they still had the wind up them.

Jesus sees some mates (Mark 16:9-14)[3]

Well, it turned out that one of the Marys (who Jesus had fixed

3 Most Bible experts actually reckon the next page or so is an add-on, included perhaps because the final bits of Mark's effort seemed to have

up from a pack of evil forces) was in fact the first one who caught up with the return of Jesus. When she'd seen him she went and told the rest of the mates, who were still quite cut up about what had happened to Jesus. When Mary told them he was alive and she'd had a coffee with him, their immediate disbelieving response was, 'Yeah, right, pull the other one!'

Not long after that, Jesus caught up with a couple of them out strolling in the countryside, appearing to them in a different sort of format. These two guys went and told the rest of them, and their immediate disbelieving response was – you guessed it – 'Yeah, right, pull the other one!'

Shortly thereafter Jesus popped in on the eleven mates (twelve minus Jude, you'll recall) while they were having a feed. 'You faithless dorks!' he told them. 'You don't even trust your mates who I've nattered with. Sigh!'

Jesus' parting shot to his mates (Mark 16:15–20)

Jesus then gave them something to do. 'What I want you to do is head out of here, and I want you to go far as – and then some. To the very ends of the earth – Albania to Zimbabwe, and every- where else in between too. I want you to give them all the good oil – the stuff I've been telling you about. Anyone who takes it on board and gets dunked in the creek – well, they'll be sweet as. And anyone who doesn't go for it – well, they're going to end up getting a *real* hard time.'

Jesus wrapped up his parting shot. 'The blokes (and of course blokesses) who sign up on this stuff – well, they'll be able to get rid of those no-good spiritual forces, and also speak in a range of languages. Snakes won't rattle them, no fear! Even the odd drop of poison won't cause them too much concern. And when they put a caring hand on those who are crook, they'll be back on their feet quick as you wouldn't know it.'

---

got lost. Matt and Luke, two of the other writers, have some of this stuff in their versions.

That being said, Jesus just sort of lifted off, really, heading for heaven to catch up with God, who was his old man, you'll recall.

That left his mates with something to do, for sure. So they got up, went out and started on the job – telling everyone the good news. And they knew God was with them, that's for sure, because all sorts of real good stuff happened along the way, adding a decent validity to what they were saying. Cool, eh?

Part Two

What Jesus' Mates Got Up To

Part One told the story of Jesus and what he did and that sort of stuff. When he'd moved on to another plane, it was time for his mates to do something. They'd seen all the action, and what's even better, they'd believed it, plus all that Jesus had told them. Luke, a medic by background, wrote one of the accounts which are generally called Gospels (we used some of his stuff in the prequel). However, most of what we used in Part I was from the young guy Mark who people reckon was 'first off the mark' with his Gospel. Anyhow, after all the effort of writing their Gospels, Matthew and Mark hung up their pens and retired as published authors. Luke decided to continue the narrative, giving a rundown on what Jesus' mates got up to. He wrote it for his friend Theo, as he'd previously done for his Gospel bit. So that's the bloke he addresses right at the start — you don't actually get to hear of old Theo again after that. Now read on.

Chapter 1

JESUS SETS THEM TO WORK

Jesus moves up (Acts 1:1-11)

Let's start with a bit of background, Theo me old mate. You will recall my first literary effort was all about the stuff that Jesus did. It started, like, right from when he was born, included all the rough stuff, getting nailed and all, then coming back alive and proving that to plenty of mates. Before his upwards disappearance, he was around for a bonus forty days, continuing the theme of God's great outfit and giving his mates a few final pointers.

On one particular occasion when they were having a feed, Jesus told his mates, 'I suggest you hang around these parts until the second act – that's when God's promised gift is going to turn up.' Jesus continued, 'Remember what I told you – whereas old John dunked you in the creek, God's going to get you totally full of his Spirit, eh? Watch this space!'

Well, the bros were together one evening, and they asked

Jesus, 'Mate, is this all about getting rid of the invaders from here? Cos it's about time.'

Jesus replied to them, 'Sorry lads, the timing for that sort of stuff is a bit out of reach for you. It's actually in God's department. But what I can tell you, which I reckon you'll like, is that fairly soon you're going to get totally powered up when God's Spirit comes on you. And you know what? You'll be telling, like, everybody about me and stuff. Right here on the home patch, to the near neighbours, to those across the border, and man, even right down as far as New Zealand – once they've got a few permanent residents.'

When he'd said that, he disappeared straight off into the clouds. They were still staring open-mouthed when a couple of blokes in white gear stood right by them. 'You guys,' these blokes enquired, 'what have you got your beady eyes fixed up there for? Because that self-same Jesus is one day going to make a return visit in substantially the same sort of way he took off.'

Replacing Jude, the ex-treasurer (Acts 1:12-26)

Jesus' mates went down from the hill and walked all the way to the city – and a good day's stroll it was too. They went back to their pad and sat down in the lounge. For your info, the eleven of them were Pete, John, James and Andrew, Phil and Tom, Bart and Matt, the other James (Alf's lad), Simon and Jude (a different one from the right sod who'd done Jesus in). Well, this lot did an amount of praying, they did – not just them, there was a fair group of women too, including Mary (Jesus' mum) and his bros.

One day when 120 of them had got together, Pete spoke to them all: 'Way back, old David predicted exactly the scenario we've found ourselves in. He particularly referred to Jude when he sold Jesus down the line. You'll recall that with the proceeds he got from selling off Jesus, Jude bought a bit of real estate, tripped over while surveying it, and had his guts explode all over the place. Yuk! Everybody round and about heard about it, and it became known locally as "the Bloody Paddock". Anyhow, old David referred to this, suggesting it would be a fairly good idea if nobody took up residence on that particular patch. Now, of course, Jude used to be one of the team, and old David proposed that at such time we ought to bring on a substitute. This is how I reckon we should do it. Pick one of the guys who's been part of the show right from when John was dunking people in the creek to when Jesus disappeared up yonder last week. One further requirement: he's gotta be one who saw Jesus after he came up alive and all, OK?'

In a sort of democratic way, Pete called for nominations. There were just two: a bloke called Joe (a.k.a. Justin) and another Matt. Then they said, 'Hey God, we've got these two jokers, which particular one do *you* reckon we should pick to take over from the late Jude who right now is taking part in his just deserts?' What they then actually did was take a gamble on God's pick – and it was Matt who got the job. So the team was topped up to twelve again.

Jesus' mates get all fired up (Acts 2:1–13)

Time for another of the regular annual parties, and Pentecost was the name of this particular celebration. They were having one of their usual get-togethers when there was, like, this humungous wind sweeping in and round the house they were parked in. Then what looked like little bits of fire came and landed on each of them. Cool! God's Spirit filled up each one of them, and they began yabbering in an assorted collection of different languages as God's Spirit let them. Awesome!

On that occasion there was a bunch of God's mates from loads of different countries who'd turned up in town for the Pentecost celebration. When they heard the kerfuffle they were fair surprised, what with everyone's language being covered by one or other of the blokes. 'Good grief!' they said. 'Isn't this just a bunch of locals? If so, would you care to explain how we can actually hear them spouting in *our* particular lingo? We've come from just about *everywhere* – and we hear them telling us about God and stuff in our very own language. What the blazes can this all mean?' Some of the passers-by, however, thought they had it sussed, albeit differently. 'They're just pissed,' they reckoned.

Pete tells it like it is (Acts 2:14–41)

Pete saw an opportune moment: 'Listen everybody! I'd like to offer a word of explanation at this particular point. These guys have *not* in fact had too much to drink, as some of you have suggested. For crying out loud, it's not even morning smoko time. In fact, as that writer Joe said yonks ago, "When things are heading towards the finale," according to God (as per Joe), "I'm going to pour out my Spirit on everybody. You're going to speak some amazing stuff, all of ya! The young lads and the old guys, all of you are going to have some fairly interesting dreams and stuff. Anyone, everyone who is on my side, they're going to get prophetic, eh? I'll prove it too – blood and fire and thunder and all sorts of special effects. The sun is going to look black, the moon's going to go like blood before the great day when I'll get everything sorted. And everyone who says they know me, they'll be sweet as."'

Pete continued his challenge: 'I suggest you listen to what I've got to say to you guys. Jesus was a bloke that God sent here to do all sorts of fantastic things round and about. God gave him to you as a gift. But what did you do? You miserable sods, you strung him up for his trouble, that's what you did! But that wasn't it by half. God got him alive again! No way would some grave hold him down.

'It's like when way back David reckoned that he always knew God would keep an eye on him. As a result, Dave had a fair degree of confidence – enthusiasm even – and he knew too that he wouldn't just up and die and rot in a no-point sort of way. Matter of fact, of course old Dave *did* die, and his grave is not too far from where I'm standing at this particular spot. Point is, however, he had an idea of what was ahead, and that God in fact had promised that one of Dave's great-great-great-great-whatever grandsons would end up kingpin. Old Dave could see that this guy, who of course turned out to be Jesus, wouldn't end up staying dead, no way. Up he'd come from his grave – and we all know that, eh? Now Jesus has given us God's Spirit that we'd been hearing about – and you can see how that's turned out today. Good, eh? So I'm telling you this, and it's non-negotiable: that bloke Jesus that you strung up, well, God's made him the boss of everything. *Everything*!'

Well, that set the people going, didn't it. 'Pete, me old mate,' they said, 'what do you reckon we ought to do?'

'Simple!' he told them. 'Turn your lives in a new direction, and get dunked in the creek in the name of Jesus Christ to get your bad stuff cleaned up. And then you'll get God's Spirit too. This ain't just for you – it's for your kids too, and people way out in the blue yonder. In fact, anyone who hears what God's got to say to them.' Pete had a fair few other things to say to the crowd as well. Like: 'I'd suggest you cut yourselves off from the pointlessness and stupidity of the current generation.' Well, Pete's words sure struck home – on that occasion some three grand signed up and were dunked in the creek.

All about being pretty good mates (Acts 2:42–47)

The new recruits, well, they hung on every word Pete and his eleven colleagues told them. They all got together fairly regularly, they prayed and had some good feeds. Everyone was pretty blown away – all the fantastic stuff the team was getting up to. They lived in a fairly communal sort of way too – none of the 'what's yours is yours and what's mine's me own' sort of approach, anything but. All their stuff was pooled, you could help yourself to whatever you needed. Every day they got together down at the temple. And every day they also got together in everyone's pad and had a great feed. Fairly cheerful they were too, thanking God regularly. The general public saw that they were all right, no worries. And the show kept on growing.

The differently-abled bloke (Acts 3:1-11)

One afternoon Pete and John were popping down to the temple to do some praying. There was this bloke, disabled from day one, being carted down to the gate which was his location of choice for his daily begging. He saw Pete and John arriving, and thought he'd hit them up for a few bucks. Pete and John looked him straight in the eye. 'Hey mate!' said Pete. The bloke looked up, waiting for the clink of the coins. 'We ain't got a brass razoo,' Pete told him. 'However, we'd like to suggest an alternative. What we *can* offer is this: in the name of our mate JC, get on your feet and go!' This being said, Pete bent down, gave him a hand up, and wow, straight off, his feet were fixed up and he was right as. He was just about bouncing off the ceiling, he was, praising God enthusiastically. Of course, the locals recognised him, and they were fairly knocked over by what had happened to the disabled bloke. Everyone crowded around them by the temple.

Pete explains some stuff (Acts 3:12-26)

'What goes?' Pete asked them. 'Why do you think this is such a big deal? We ain't done this ourselves because we're smart as, or anything like it. No way! In fact, God, the boss of everyone from way back such as Abe, Isaac and Jake and the lot of them, he's shown up Jesus to be real good. You lot wanted him done in, you might recall – even though the judge was ready to acquit him. You said to that Pilate fellow, "You can forget him! Let that murderer bloke go free instead," eh? So you wasted Jesus, didn't you? But God wasn't going to keep him dead, no sir! And that brings us to the present set of circumstances – it's faith in JC that has got this disabled bloke (who you all know fairly well) running around like nothing on earth. He trusted in Jesus, eh? And that's been plenty good enough for him. OK, OK, I know you really didn't have a clue what you were up to when you did all that to Jesus, you and your leaders. That's pretty obvious. But in fact God knew this would happen – he said so yonks back through some of his mates, he knew JC was going to get a hard time.

'What you've got to do is fairly straightforward in essence. Turn your lives around. Sign up with God so all your bad stuff gets forgotten, you get fantastically sorted out, and Jesus will be your mate.'

Peter carried on: 'Jesus is going to continue to be based in heaven until God's finally got everything sorted out. We've known that of course since way back – we got it from all those mates of God who wrote wise stuff. Take Moses, for example. He said that God was going to get somebody up and running a bit like himself, someone who'd be well worth the time of day. In fact, old Mo reckoned, if you ignored this particular guy your life would be worth stuff all. Matter of fact, all the prophet types from Sam onwards, they've all given a fair sort of indicator on what's going to happen right now. And you guys are the beneficiaries of all of that – all the agreements that God signed off on with your ancestors. God told Abe way back that his eventual offspring would cause a significant degree of good stuff for everyone everywhere. So God, by getting JC back from the dead, has organised it that you lot will have the first shot at getting in good with God. This involves, like I said, getting your lives changed around a fair bit. Got that?'

Pete and John get taken in (Acts 4:1-22)

While Pete and John were nattering with the crowd on these particular themes, who should turn up but some of the old God squad, with a few members of security for support. As you might imagine, they were less than impressed with what our blokes were speaking about, including talking about Jesus getting up and about after being thoroughly dead. They stuck Pete and John in handcuffs and threw them in the slammer, what with it being evening and all, and the court closed for the day. But that didn't stop the crowd signing up – by now there were around five grand all told.

Next day, a bit of a consultation was called – anyone and everyone who was someone was there, including every last significant person from the religious establishment. Pete and John were dragged in from the cells. 'Under whose auspices do you suggest you are operating?' the religious leaders asked them.

Pete, all stoked up on God's Spirit, took the stand. 'You guys, leaders of the whole shooting box you are. You're asking us if we wouldn't mind explaining how and why we gave a spot of assistance to that disabled bloke, and got him thoroughly fixed up. Listen you guys, I'll give it to you straight. We did it in the name of JC, that's who. In case you'd forgotten, he was the one you strung up, but God got him out of the grave and alive again, no worries. Jesus is, like, the most important bit of the building that got the heave from the builders, but now he's the foundation of everything. There's no one else that can save you, nobody! It's by him alone that God's provided the wherewithal for you to get off the hook.'

Now, the gathered religious types were a bit blown away by Pete and John saying this stuff. After all, weren't they really just a couple of fairly ignorant peasants? Ignorant peasants, for all that, who'd hung around as part of Jesus' crowd. Problem was, the bloke formerly known as the disabled bloke, he was hanging around there fit as a fiddle for all to see. So they couldn't really object much to that, could they?

At this point they went into committee, as it were, making Pete and John stand outside. 'What the hell can we do with these guys?' they wondered. 'Everybody can see that they've done a pretty fantastic thing with that disabled bloke. But we really can't have too much of this going on, it's got the potential to get out of hand. How's this for an idea – we'll tell them to call it quits on speaking and doing stuff in that bloke Jesus' name, and if they don't listen, then they'll be in trouble big-time.'

So they got Pete and John back in the room: 'If you guys so much as speak or teach in the name of that bloke Jesus one more time, then you're in for it big-time. So you'd better watch it.'

'Oh yeah?' Pete responded. 'Look here, suss this one out. What do you reckon God's view would be on whether we obey you or him? One thing's for sure, there's no way you can shut us up on the stuff we've seen or heard.'

This put the religious leaders in a bit of a spot. They issued a few more dark threats, then let them go – not much else they could do really because everybody was enthusiastically telling God he'd done such a great job. And that was made more significant by the fact that the formerly disabled bloke was more than forty – quite old in the particular circumstances.

Everyone prays a bit (Acts 4:23-31)

Pete and John took advantage of their freedom and headed back to their mates, giving them a bit of a rundown on what had happened and what the cops and all had said. And their mates, they spoke to God, they did. 'Hey God,' they said. 'You're the one who made this whole show. Way back you said some things via old Dave, you did. Stuff like, "What's all the fuss about? Why all the fights and scraps which are not very effectual? You world-leader types, plotting against God and his special bloke!" Hey God, you know that Herod and that bloke Pilate, they and a whole bunch from everywhere set up your guy Jesus. Matter of fact, you'd already seen it would happen, eh God? Well, what we'd like to ask you God, is that you'll please take note of what the religious establishment is threatening. You see, we'd like our mates to be able to enthusiastically tell everyone what side their bread's buttered on.' When they'd finished talking with God the whole place got shooken up. God's Spirit was in all of them, and they talked about God's stuff fairly confidently.

Everyone shares a bit (Acts 4:32-36)

All the new bunch of believers were in quite good with each other, no scrapping or anything. No one fenced in his own stuff to keep others out – everything belonged to everybody. With a fair amount of influence the leading blokes continued to spout about Jesus coming alive again and the significance thereof. And everyone and everything was pretty good all round as a result. Nobody went short of a thing. From time to time, whenever anybody sold their houses or empty sections, well, they brought the dosh and gave it to the leading blokes – who dished it out wherever and however needed. Here's an example for you. There was a bloke called Joe (a.k.a. Barney) from across the waves in Cyprus – he'd had this paddock which he put on the market. It sold, and he gave the proceeds to the leaders to deal with. Good, eh?

Telling porkies (Acts 5:1-11)

Now, there was a bloke called Ananias married to a woman called Sapphira. Since these names aren't very common these days we'll call 'em Andy and Sophie for short. Anyhow, they were good Christians, and they had an acre or two to spare, so they sold it off. The idea was of course to give the money to the team. But this is where things go wrong. Andy, with the full knowledge of Sophie, handed over less than the total proceeds (but claiming it was the lot), hanging on to a bit himself for a rainy day. Pete's no fool, though. 'Andy,' he says, 'what a proper dickhead you are. How come the evil one got you to have a shot at fooling God's Spirit and retaining a cut for yourself? You're an absolute dork, you know – cos when you look at it, the particular acreage was yours right from the start, you could have done what you liked with it. Even when you hocked it off, you could still have done what you liked with the money. So what the hell caused you to do such an absolutely mad thing, making yourself out to be such a great guy but in fact endeavouring to pull the wool over our eyes?

You might think you can fool us, but you can't fool God, no sir!'

Now this was somewhat embarrassing, and Andy was a bit stumped. He basically dropped down dead, just like that. When word got out and about, well, it sort of put the wind up everyone. The guys on duty came in and took ex-Andy outside, where they buried him quick-like.

Well, a couple of hours later, in walked Sophie – she'd been out of circulation briefly and hadn't caught up with the fact that her other half had karked it. So Pete said to her, 'Hey Sophie, the money that Andy dropped round, I'd be glad of some confirmation – is that the full price you got for your bit of land?'

'Bang on,' replied Sophie.

'You stupid cow!' Pete told her. 'On what particular basis do you think you can stick it to God? Hear those footsteps outside? They're from the blokes who've just buried your old man. They're looking for the next job, and I'm afraid to say, you're it.' With that, Sophie keeled over, dead as. In came the burial party, took her out and stuck her in the hole next to her husband.

When the folks in the church, and everywhere else for that matter, heard about it, well, it sort of put double the wind up them.

Fixing up the crook (Acts 5:12-16)

Pete and his mates performed a fair few amazing things here and there among the crowds, who used to have regular get-togethers down at the temple. Others looked on and thought it was pretty all right, but were still cautious about signing up. A fair swag did sign up however, blokes and blokesses who decided to throw in their lot with Jesus and co. Good stuff was happening so much in all directions that people used to bring down their mates who were crook, hoping the shadow of Pete as he walked past would do the trick. People even came from the suburbs and beyond, all the time bringing along their mates who were a bit crook for a fix-up, plus those with the usual dark forces and stuff. Every time a coconut, no worries.

Getting a rough time (Acts 5:17–42)

Well, the religious head, him and some of his mates, they got rather hacked off with all this carry-on. So they got Pete and the team arrested and flung them in the slammer again. But you can't keep God down, can you? Cos that night one of his angel blokes came and opened the jail door and let them out, just like that. 'You guys,' the angel told them, 'get back down to the temple in the morning, and tell them all about this new life stuff, OK?'

Crack of dawn, they did just that, down to the temple yard they went and got straight back into giving the crowds the good stuff. Later on the religious boss and his mates turned up for work, called together the council for a bit of a hearing, and then summoned the Jesus gang from jail. Security went to jail, but shock, horror, it was empty. Back at the temple they reported: 'Excuse me, boss, we went to pick up the accused, the place was nice and secure as you'd expect, but when the screws opened the doors, guess who was in there? Nobody! Absolutely deserted it was.'

Now, this was a fairly unusual sort of report, and the temple guys struggled to get a handle on it. Good grief, what the heck would happen next? A fairly observant character popped in on the meeting at this point. 'Guess what?' he told them. 'Those guys you stuck in jail last night, they're out, they're here, and they're back doing their stuff again right outside.'

The security chief took a handful of his men, went outside, grabbed the boys and brought them into the meeting. They did it sort of gentle-like – they weren't wanting any rioting, no way. Straight to the council chamber, where the boss started his piece. 'I've a fair idea we told you to quit yabbering in the name of the said Jesus,' he told them. 'Yet you've continued on this lark, and you're telling everyone *we* were the ones that got Jesus strung up.'

'This needs a bit of clarification,' Pete began, on behalf of the guys. 'Our particular responsibility is to obey God rather than you lot. And it so happens that it was God – yours and mine – who got this Jesus bloke (who you guys killed) fully up and about and undead. God's promoted him to a key role as his right-hand man with particular responsibilities for sorting out and forgiving anyone from these parts. I tell you, we've seen this stuff with our very own eyes, and so has God's Spirit – in fact, this spirit character is around for anyone who's got it properly sussed.'

That rather set the cat among the pigeons – they were furious, I tell you. So much so, that they wanted to string up this lot too. But one of the officials, a bloke called Gamaliel, who was a lawyer in fact and held in fairly high regard all round, well, he called a pause in the proceedings. 'Stick those guys outside for a sec,' he instructed. So they stuck those guys outside for a sec. 'All right you fellas,' Gam told them. 'You've gotta be fairly careful what you do to these guys, eh? Some time back a bloke called Theudas (for real!) turned up in town, reckoned he was fairly special, and some four hundred blokes got signed up. Well, he got strung up, he did, and his mates took off, end of story. A bit further down the track a guy Jude from down the lake area turned up around census time. He got strung up too, his mates scattered to the four winds, same stuff, end of story. In the particular circumstances we have at this particular point in time, I reckon you should just ignore those guys. Send 'em packing! If, like in the examples I just gave you, it's just a flash in the pan, nothing will happen. If, however, God is behind this, then it's not a particularly good idea to take on God, eh? God tends to win on such occasions.'

'Fair enough,' was the general consensus from the gathered. So they got the lads back in and gave them a fair hiding to make a point. Then they told them to quit speaking in the name of their mate Jesus – and packed them off down the road.

The guys got out of there, stoked that they had had to suffer a bit on account of their mate Jesus. And you can guess what they *didn't* do – they didn't stop. No sir, every which day they carried on, telling anyone who would listen – any venue was fine – that their mate Jesus was God's number one bloke.

A good lesson in delegation (Acts 6:1-7)

Stuff kept happening, and the band of Jesus' followers just kept on getting bigger. You'll recall that they did a fair amount of communal living, sharing their stuff generously and all. Well, a bit of a hiccup occurred on ethnic lines, would you believe? The widows of Greek origin were running short compared with the local widows when it came to handing out the food parcels. So Pete and the team got everyone together for a natter.

'Listen you guys,' Pete told them, 'we've clearly got a bit of an issue here. However, in terms of our strategic purposes, it would seem a bit stupid for us leaders to quit our promo work so as we can run the food bank, eh? What I'd like to suggest is that you choose seven guys from among yourselves, blokes that have a bit of a track record and are in good on the God stuff. These blokes can take charge of the food bank and asset management in general, while we'll carry on in the spouting and yabbering department. And of course we'll keep up a fair bit of prayer too. Sound reasonable?'

Everyone thought this sounded fairly good. 'That sounds fairly good,' they responded. So they picked Steve, a bloke strong in the faith department and clearly filled up on God's Spirit. In addition there was Phil, Nic, another Nic, Timo and a couple of other blokes with unusual names. 'What do you think of this bunch?' they asked Pete and co.

'Good!' replied Pete. He and his mates prayed for them and set them to work. And this particular strategic activity turned out to be a fairly good idea as the bunch of signed-ups just kept on growing more and more. And guess what – quite a swag of those who'd been religious leaders under the old regime, they joined up too.

Chapter 2

THE STUFF STARTS GOING FURTHER

Steve – a real good bloke (Acts 6:8–15)

Now, Steve was a real good bloke in God's book, and people noticed all the good stuff he got up to. However, there was one particular bunch of guys who rather got off their bikes as far as Steve was concerned. They tried to have it out with him, but to no avail, he was smart as, and clearly had God's Spirit on his side. So what to do? On the quiet they conned a few other guys to make up stuff about Steve. 'Now, about Steve,' they'd say to whoever, 'he's been saying a few inappropriate things about God and Mo, which really isn't on, eh?' Of course, word got around, and the usual religious authorities got called in to sort it out. They pulled Steve into the courtroom, and produced a few witnesses who took the concept of truth with a considerable grain of salt.

'This bloke Steve,' they said, 'he can't help himself, he just keeps laying into the establishment, temple and all. What's more, we have him on record as saying that his mate Jesus is going to tear this place down, and then change all the traditions we've had since way back in Mo's day. This really isn't on, eh?'

The council guys, they took a fairly close look at Steve. And every last one of them reckoned old Steve looked not unlike one of those angel fellas.

Steve gives a bit of a rundown on history
(Acts 7:1–16)

Well, the boss man, he turned to Steve: 'What's your particular angle on the charges as presented? True, or a pack of lies?'

Steve saw his chance to give a bit of a rundown on history: 'Hey everyone, I've got something to say, OK? Way back, God turned up for a bit of a chinwag with old Abe, while he was still at his old pad. "I want you to pack your bags and head off to a new locale," God told Abe. "I'll tell you when you've got there, OK?" So Abe moved on, doing exactly God's bidding. When Abe's old man karked it, he moved on again to the place where we now all are, though without one bit of his own real estate. However, that ain't all – God told him he'd get a bit of land in due course, even though at that particular time Abe didn't have any kids.

'God put it to him this way: "Your descendants are going to have it tough in foreign parts – they're going to be treated as beneficiaries and overstayers and generally be kicked around by everyone for four hundred years. But I'm telling you, the nasty sods who do it to them are going to get it in the neck. Then after that, your guys are going to quit that location and come right here and be mates with me." God then instructed Abe in a particular symbolic ritual whereby they would chop off the tip of little boys' willies. The point of this practice of willy-clipping is to show God's commitment to them.'

Steve continued: 'Some time later, Abe had a son Isaac, and did the willy-clipping thing after about a week. Then Isaac in his turn had a son called Jake, and Jake had a dozen boys himself, each of whom was to father some more family lines. One of Jake's kids was a lad called Joe. Some of his bros thought Joe was a bit up himself, so they hocked him off in a foreign employment exchange. Joe thus got himself a job offshore, where he got caught up in a load of trouble. However, God didn't forget him, no way. He got him out of that – in fact, got him in good with the King of Egypt no less. Joe ended up as prime minister, would you believe, boss of most of the significant power-bases in Egypt.

'Then, oh dear, famine struck Egypt and roundabout. People starving everywhere. Real sad it was. Jake heard that you could get a bit of a feed in Egypt, so he sent some of his boys to get some. When they went back for a second lot, their bro Joe who'd put on a drama for them last time, well, he fronted up with who he actually was. Then Joe told the king about who his old man and bros were, so the king said, "Hey, they can come and live here in Egypt, no worries." So they did, and there were seventy-five of them – the whole whanau. Jake and the lads, they settled in Egypt. Lived there, died there. And they all got buried back where they'd come from.'

Steve's history lesson, Part Two (Acts 7:17–53)

'Well,' said Steve, 'some four hundred years down the track, it was time for God's promise to Abe about the land and stuff to finally happen. It came about like this. All their descendants had bred considerably, there was now a whole heap of them. The monarch person of the time didn't know much history, so the story of Joe and co meant stuff all to him. This particular king was a right sod, he was. He did lots of awful stuff, the worst of which was to make the mums toss out their newborns – rotten, eh?

'Around now, old Mo was born, and I tell you, he was no ordinary kid. For his first three months he was brought up at home, regular-like. Then with the rule about tossing out the nippers, well I never, it was the king's very own daughter that found him and brought him up. Well, he went to all the Egyptian schools and stuff, and he was a fairly smart bloke, he was. One day Mo turned forty, as you do, and he decided to visit some of his real whanau. On this particular occasion he saw an Egyptian doing the dirty on one of them. That was no good, no sir. So Mo killed this Egyptian guy, just like that.'

Steve carried on with the history: 'Old Mo reckoned people would know he was going to get them out of the hole they were in, but they weren't all on the same page in the hymn book, as it were. This showed up next day when Mo found a couple of his lot scrapping. "Come on lads," he told them, "you're supposed to be mates. So what's the fuss about?" The guy who was winning the scrap turned to Mo. "And just who the hell do you think you are?" he demanded. "Is it your big plan to do me in just like you did the Egyptian yesterday, eh?" Now, this sort of put the wind up Mo, he took to his heels and checked in as a new immigrant in another place a safe distance away. While there, he got himself a woman and had a couple of sons.

'Time passed, forty years in fact,' Steve told his listeners. 'One day old Mo was out in the desert near a mountain when this angel turned up, right in the middle of this bit of bush that was on fire. Well, old Mo could hardly believe his eyes. He went up closer to see if he could suss it out. From the middle of the bush he heard a voice – it was God! "Hey man," said God. "I'm the God for Abe, Isaac, Jake and all." Mo, he shook like a leaf he did, and didn't dare look too close. "Hey you, take off your shoes. The place where you're standing is a fairly sacred place, you know. Now, I want to explain a few things to you. For sure, I've seen me mates and the hard time they've been having. I'm come to get them out of here. And this involves *you* mate, back to Egypt with ya!"

'Now,' said Steve, 'this was of course the self-same Mo that went hiding in the desert when the two guys fighting forty years back asked who the hell he thought he was. Well, here he was now, heading back to Egypt to get them all out of that place – and this mission started with God and the angel who was in that burning bush. So anyhow, Mo got them all out of Egypt, doing some fancy tricks along the way.

'They went down to the Red Sea, and crossed that, then spent forty years wandering around in the desert. Mo said to them all, "One of these days God's going to give you another clever joker a bit like me, and he's going to be one of our lot too." Yep, Mo was in the desert, speaking with that angel fellow, getting some good tips to pass on to us and all. Sad thing is, our ancestors wouldn't have a bar of it. They told him where he could stick it, and wished they were back in Egypt – short memories they had, for sure.'

Steve continued the story of Mo and his crew: 'Next up, they said to Aaron (Mo's kid bro): "Mate, we want decent gods that we can *see*. As for old Mo, we wouldn't have a clue where he is right now. Let's make some kind of statue – yep, in the form of a calf, eh?" Which they did. They honoured this stupid statue and brought it gifts and all, partying in its honour.

'God, however, he was *not* impressed, no sir. "Stuff it!" he said. "If that's what you really want, go for it, worship all that nonsense!" Matter of fact, this is written up in one of the books of the wise guys where he says, "Hey guys, did you really bring me gifts of meat and stuff during those forty years wandering around in the desert? No way, you were too tied up making up all these fancy gods of various descriptions. All right, you're getting banished you are, way way away from here." And they were, weren't they?

'All along, these guys actually had a sort of portable church thingy – all specially made up by Mo and co, according to God's specs. Josh and his mates further down the track, well, they had it too when they moved into these parts after chasing out the previous inhabitants. It continued in current usage right till Dave became king, when he decided to provide a bit more of a permanent structure. Dave was in fairly good with God, he was, but it was actually his lad Solomon, when he was doing the king thing, who was the one who built a decent place for it all. However, it's worth noting that God doesn't actually live in houses that we build, it's not like that. As one of those old wise guys put it, quoting God: "I'm actually resident in heaven, and it's like, I put my feet up on earth. So what particular type of abode have you got planned for me? Where do you reckon I should put my feet up? Don't you twig – I've already got that all sussed." '

At this point Steve really laid into his listeners: 'You pack of stupid ignorant gits! You're all thick as, just like your ancestors. You guys just never seem to get it. You just will not hear what God's Spirit is up to, eh? All God's special reps from way back – every one of them – you stuck it to them. Anyone who said anything about God's special bloke – well, you took them out, didn't you? And now, final straw, you've actually done in the actual bloke God has been telling us about for yonks. You killed him! Yep, *you* – the ones who've had *all* the opportunities, advance knowledge and all. You've blown it!' Steve concluded.

Steve gets stoned (with stones) (Acts 7:54–60)

Well I never, that set them off like nothing on earth. They let Steve know exactly what they thought of him. And it was less than complimentary, that's for sure. Steve, however, no worries, he was filled with God's Spirit, he was. He could actually see heaven, and see God and Jesus right there. 'Hey everyone,' he said. 'I can see heaven, and there's God and Jesus right there.' Man, the crowd went berserk with him. They charged into him, dragged him out of town and heaved these enormous rocks at him. To make the task easier they took off their jackets and asked this bloke called Saul to keep an eye on them. Meanwhile, as the rocks were crashing all over and into Steve, he calmly prayed.

'Hey Jesus,' he said, 'I think I'm heading to your department.' He collapsed onto the ground. 'Jesus,' he cried, 'please don't hold this against these guys.' And then he was dead. Saul, the guy watching the jackets, he was there, enthusiastically adding his endorsement to the whole proceedings.

Quite a bit of emigration (Acts 8:1–8)

That was the beginning of a particularly hard time for all the blokes and blokesses of the new church outfit. Apart from the dozen leading guys, the rest got scattered all over the show. Meantime, some of Steve's caring mates gave him a decent burial. They were really cut up about what had happened to him.

But as for Saul, he was wild as. He went hither and yon grabbing anyone and everyone that believed in this Jesus man, and sticking them in jail. This new church thing, there was no way *that* was going to last, in his view.

Guess what? Those who got scattered took their faith and practice with them wherever they happened to turn up. Take Phil for example – he went down across the border to this place called Samaria and told them there all about God's number one bloke. When people heard him and saw the special stuff he did, they listened all the more. Evil forces, they just took off, they did. Anyone who was crook – any and every disability – well, they got fixed up. Everyone was over the moon.

Simon has big ideas (Acts 8:9–25)

In town there was a guy called Simon who'd practised black magic, and the locals thought he was pretty good too. He actually was a bit up himself with it all, cos everything they said about him went to his head. But even though he'd been at it a fair while, when Phil came talking about JC and stuff, everyone forgot about Simon. Instead, they got themselves dunked to show they were part of the Jesus set. And guess what – same happened to the Simon bloke. Yeah! He became like Phil's shadow, rocked out of his boots by what he saw.

Meanwhile, back at the HQ for the new church, the leading blokes heard that the guys in Samaria had bought into JC and stuff. So they sent Pete and John to check them out. Now, these Samaria guys, they'd been dunked like everyone else in Jesus' name, but they'd gone a bit short in the bit about getting God's Spirit. 'No worries,' said Pete and John. They stuck their hands on them, prayed for them then and there, asking that they'd get God's Spirit in them – and they did!

This struck Simon (the bloke I'd just mentioned) as being fairly smart. He could see this having some commercial potential, and offered them a good financial incentive if he could get in on the act. 'I'd be fairly keen on getting in on the act,' Simon told them. 'I also want people to get God's Spirit when I stick my hands on them.'

'You *what*?' asked Pete. 'Well, you can go to hell and take your filthy money with you too if you reckon you can do this stuff commercially. I tell you, you've got to get things a bit better sussed with God than you currently have. Change your crooked ways mate, and ask God to let you off. Maybe he will even – because right now you're useless as.'

Simon responded, 'Um, yeah, see your point. I'd be obliged if you'd put in a good word for me with God so that none of your suggestions about me going to hell will in fact happen.'

Pete and John did some more preaching about Jesus here and there, then they headed back to their home patch.

Phil and the Ethiopian bloke (Acts 8:26–40)

Meantime, an angel had a word with Phil. 'Hey Phil,' he said. 'I want you to head south from here, go down the desert road in the direction of Gaza.' So Phil did. He headed off down the road, and he ran into this guy from Ethiopia who was a eunuch (meaning he'd had his balls cut off, often done in those days for a particular branch of the workforce). This Ethiopian was a VIP back home where he had a fairly significant role in the Treasury. Now he'd made a trip to Jerusalem for worship purposes, and on his way back home he was sitting in his vehicle reading the good book, and some stuff by old Isaiah in particular. God's Spirit said to Phil, 'Hey Phil, wander over near that guy in the chariot, there's a good lad.' So Phil, being a good lad, did. He couldn't help overhearing the bloke reading from the said Isaiah bit.

'Excuse me, any idea of what that stuff is all about?' Phil asked him.

'How the blazes can I have any idea, unless someone actually gives me a bit of background?' replied the Ethiopian. The particular bit he was reading went like this: 'Just like a lamb at the works, or a sheep about to be shorn, says nothing, so neither did he. He was completely humiliated, he was, not a scrap of justice he got. And how can you talk about his kids? His life was snuffed out.' The Ethiopian turned to Phil. 'Tell me mate,' he asked him, 'who's this guy on about – himself or some other bloke?'

Phil saw his opportunity, and using that particular bit from the good book he told the Ethiopian all the stuff there was to know about Jesus. As they cruised on down the road, they passed a pond. 'Hey Phil,' said the Ethiopian, 'here's a pond with enough H_2O for dunking – how about it, eh?' They stopped the chariot, got off and down into the drink, where Phil dunked him. As they got out of the water, God's Spirit sort of zapped Phil and he disappeared just like that. The Ethiopian character couldn't work out what had happened to his new mate Phil, but whatever, he carried on down the road, and he was sure stoked he was.

Phil, meantime, turned up at another town down the road, and he carried on telling everyone about JC all the way down to where he was planning on putting his feet up for a bit. Cool, eh?

Chapter 3

SAUL (A.K.A. PAUL) SWAPS SIDES

Saul and the special effects (Acts 9:1-9)

Remember that young bloke Saul? Well, he was still on the case, going hammer and tongs to take out as many of the Jesus gang as he could. He fronted up to the kingpin of the religious leaders and asked for an intro to the more junior leaders down the road in Damascus. His idea – if he found any of the Jesus bunch, he'd take 'em in and cart 'em back to Jerusalem.

Well, Saul got on the road, and was getting fairly close to his destination, when all of a sudden there was this humungously bright light in the sky. Knocked him straight to the ground, it did, wow! Then a voice: 'Hey Saul, what's the story? Why do you keep hounding me like you're doing?'

'May I ask who's speaking, please?' Saul replied, more than a little baffled.

'It's me, Jesus, the one you're trying to do in,' came the reply. 'Now listen to me. Get yourself up, head into the city as planned, then you'll get your further instructions.' Well, Saul's mates, they were gobsmacked. They heard all that was going on, but couldn't see zilch. Saul, meantime, he got himself up, opened his eyes, but that did a fat lot of good – because he couldn't see if you'd paid him. His mates took him on down the road to Damascus. For the next three days he was blind as a bat, and never had a feed, not even a drink.

Andy gives Saul a few tips (Acts 9:10-22)

In Damascus there was this bloke Ananias. (Same name, but not the same bloke as karked it when he told some porkies a few pages back – we'll call this guy Andy too.) Well, Andy had this dream one night. Jesus said to him in this dream, 'Hey Andy!'

'Yep? What do you want, boss?' Andy replied.

Jesus gave him his mission: 'I want you to head to this B&B owned by a bloke called Jude, down on Straight Street you'll find it. Ask for a bloke there by the name of Saul, originally from Tarsus. He's doing a spot of praying, actually. While praying he's had this dream of a bloke called Andy coming to pray for him so that he gets his 20/20 vision back. OK?'

'Hey Jesus, you've *got* to be joking. The grapevine tells me this bloke has done a fair degree of damage to your guys up in the big smoke. Matter of fact, he's got approval to come and do the same to us lot down here – any of us in your outfit are going to get thrown in the slammer. Are you really sure about this idea of yours?'

'Too right,' Jesus replied. 'This guy, believe it or not, is going to be my special agent and represent me in all sorts of places with all sorts of influential types. I'm going to point out to him that he's going to have a fairly hard time doing stuff on my behalf too.'

Well, what could Andy do? He followed instructions, of course, exactly as told. Turned up at Saul's place, stuck his hands on Saul, and said, 'Saul, me old mate. Jesus – the self-same bloke that you met up with on the way into town – well, he's sent me to fix up your vision and see that you get his Spirit.' Quick as a flash, something fell off Saul's eyes, and his look-see department was right as. Up he got, dunked he got, had a feed, and felt a bit stronger too. He got introduced to some of the mates there in Damascus, and before you know it, he was out there telling everyone that Jesus is God's number one bloke.

Everyone was absolutely blown away by this. 'Wow!' they all said. 'Is this for real? Ain't he the bloke that was doing all our mates in, down there in Jerusalem? Good grief, didn't he come down to these parts to do the same to us?'

But as for Saul, no worries, he just kept on getting better and better in the preaching thing, and he had all the local religious types totally blown away with his telling them that Jesus was God's special bloke. Cool!

The 'What Jesus' Mates Got Up To' story continues on with Saul (soon to be known as Paul) and the other blokes taking the story of Jesus and his life and doings and death and non-death all over the show. As we've seen, Paul had been a right miserable sod to the Jesus team ever since kick-off. But talk about changing sides in a big way — over the next umpteen years Paul was the best advocate for the cause by a long shot. People kept signing up, Paul kept getting thrown in jail, beaten up, shipwrecked and all. And the Jesus crowd kept on growing. Great story — you can find it in any Bible in any bookshop, online, anywhere. (Note: some Bibles don't tell it in quite the Kiwi way, but it's still pretty all right, eh?)

Where you'll find stuff in *The Kiwi Bible*